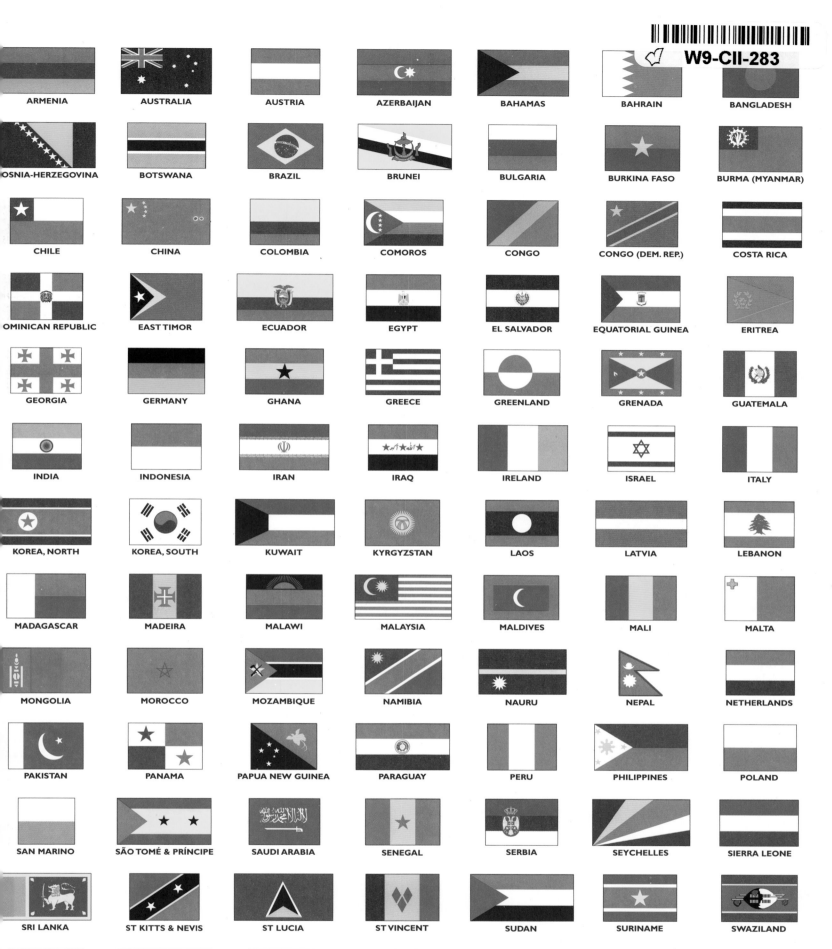

GRAMERCY FAMILY WORLD ATLAS

Contents

CITY CENTRE MAPS – KEY TO SYMBOLS

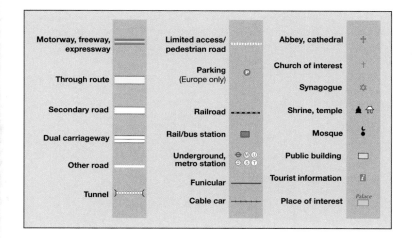

Motorway, freeway, expressway	Limited access/ pedestrian road	Abbey, cathedral	†
Through route	Parking (Europe only)	Church of interest	†
Secondary road	Railroad	Synagogue	✡
		Shrine, temple	⛩
Dual carriageway	Rail/bus station	Mosque	☾
Other road	Underground, metro station	Public building	▢
	Funicular	Tourist information	🅸
Tunnel	Cable car	Place of interest	*Palace* ▢

This 2007 edition is published by Gramercy Books, an imprint of Random House Value Publishing, a division of Random House, Inc., New York, by arrangement with Philip's.

Gramercy is a registered trademark and the colophon is a trademark of Random House, Inc.

Random House
New York · Toronto · London · Sydney · Auckland
www.randomhouse.com

Printed and bound in Hong Kong

A catalog record for this title is available from the Library of Congress.

ISBN: 978-0-517-23005-3

10 9 8 7 6 5 4 3 2 1

CITY CENTRE MAPS – Cartography by Philip's
Page iii, Dublin: The town plan of Dublin is based on Ordnance Survey Ireland by permission of the Government Permit Number 8097. © Ordnance Survey Ireland and Government of Ireland.

Ordnance Survey® Page iii, Edinburgh, and page iv, London: This product includes mapping data licensed from Ordnance Survey® with the permission of the Controller of Her Majesty's Stationery Office. © Crown copyright 2006. All rights reserved. Licence number 100011710.

Vector data: Courtesy of Gräfe and Unser Verlag GmbH, München, Germany (city centre maps of Bangkok, Mexico City, Singapore, Sydney and Tokyo).

GRAMERCY BOOKS
NEW YORK

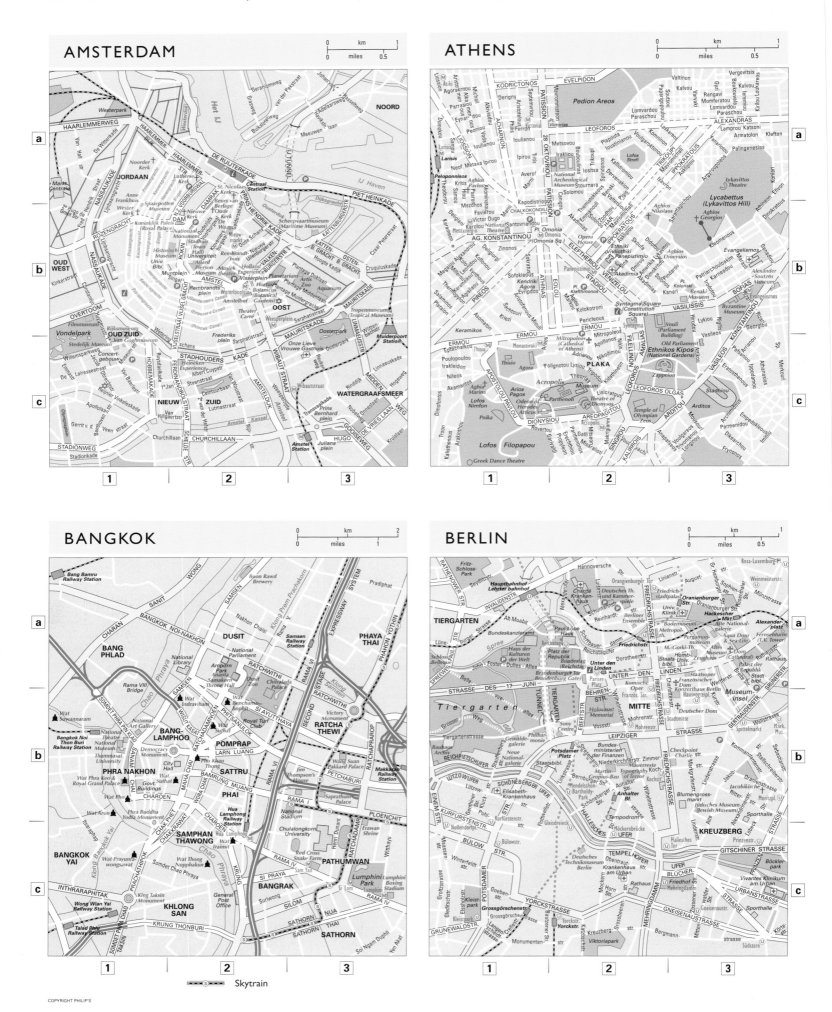

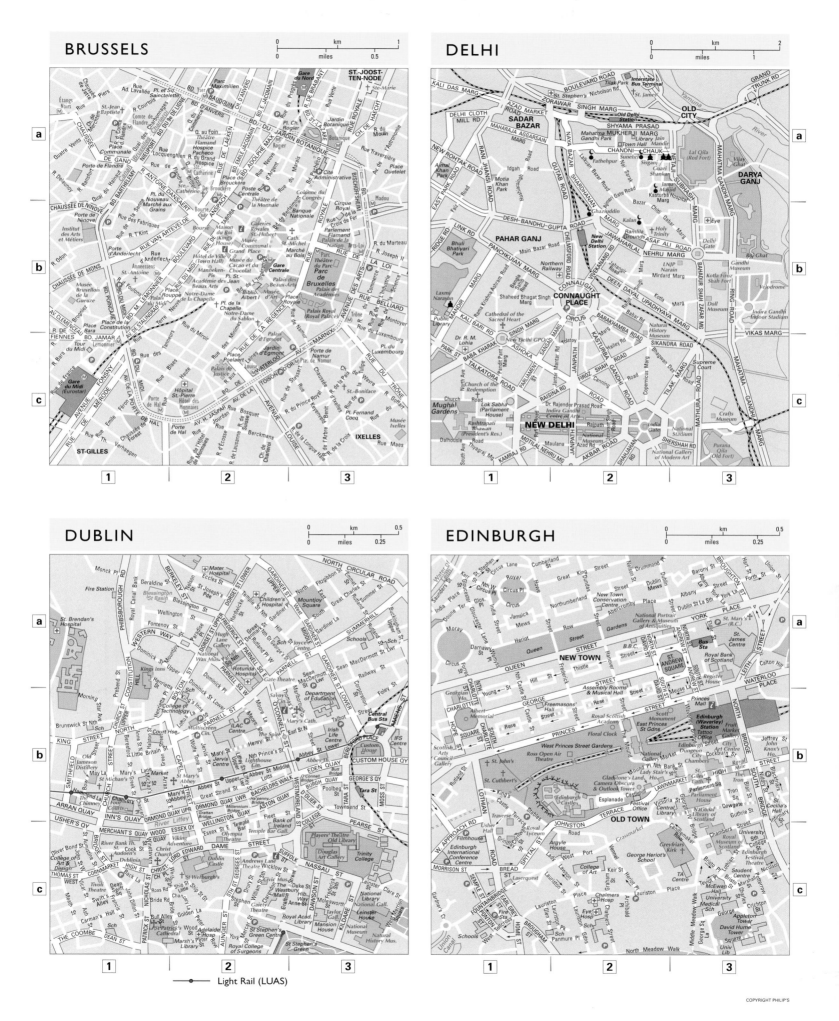

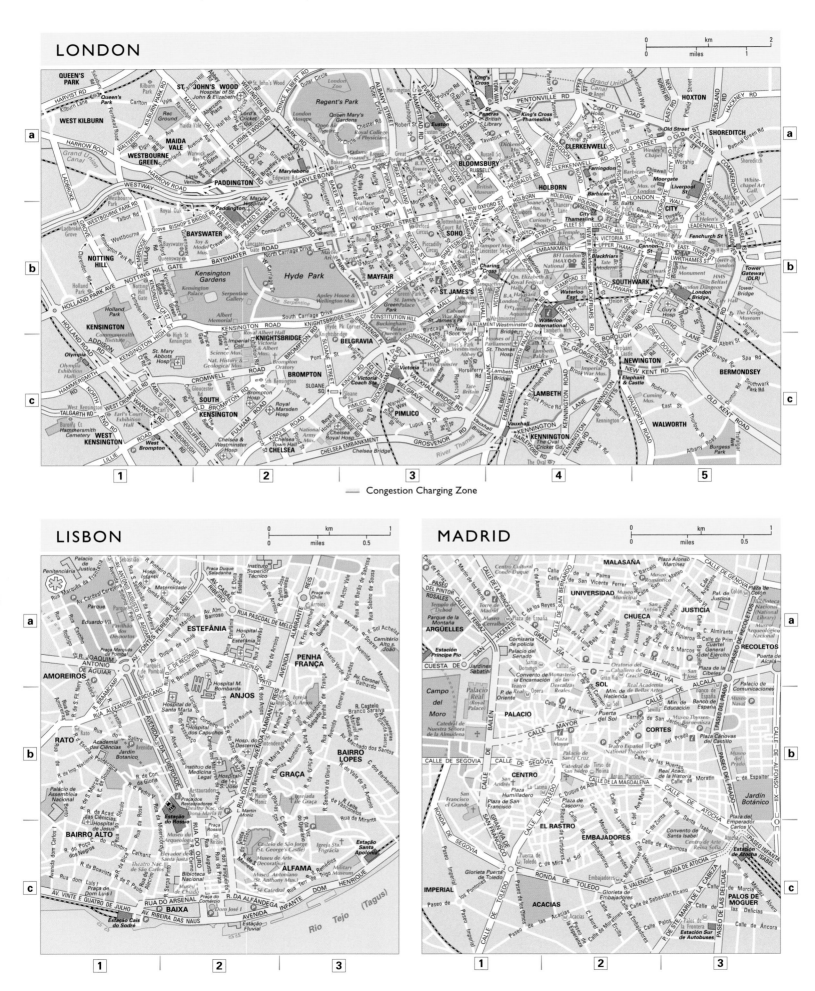

LONDON

Congestion Charging Zone

LISBON

MADRID

MEXICO CITY

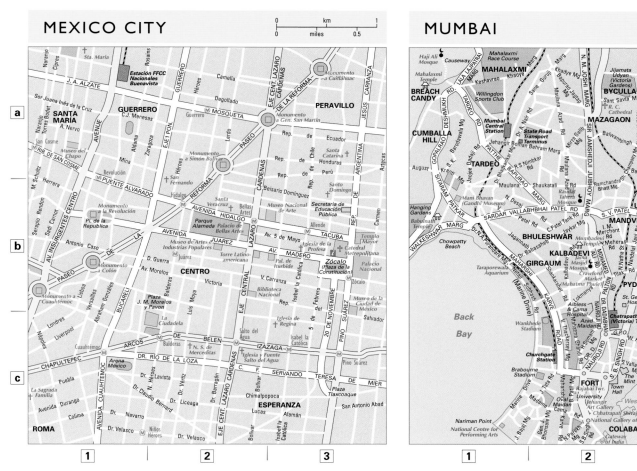

MUMBAI

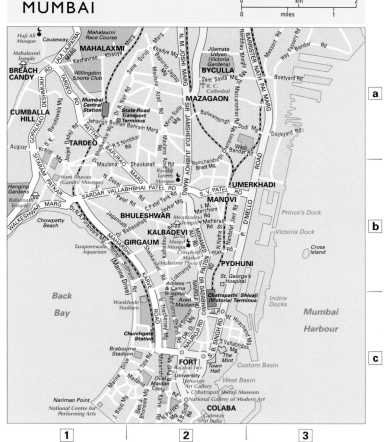

NEW YORK

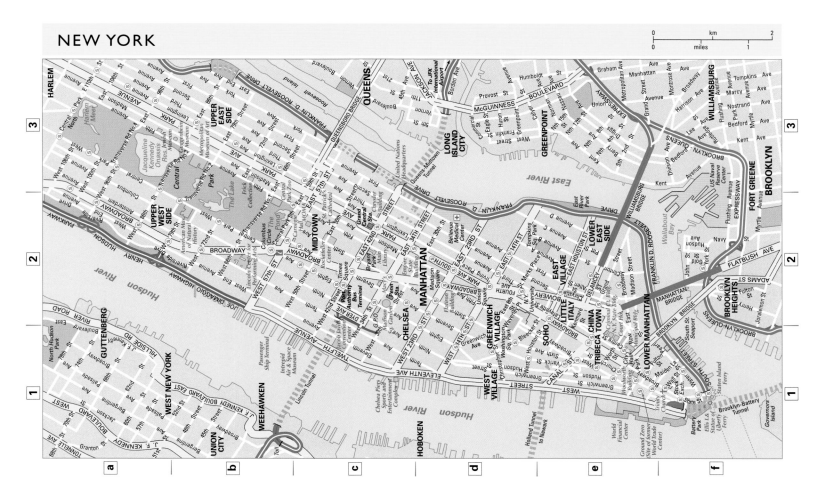

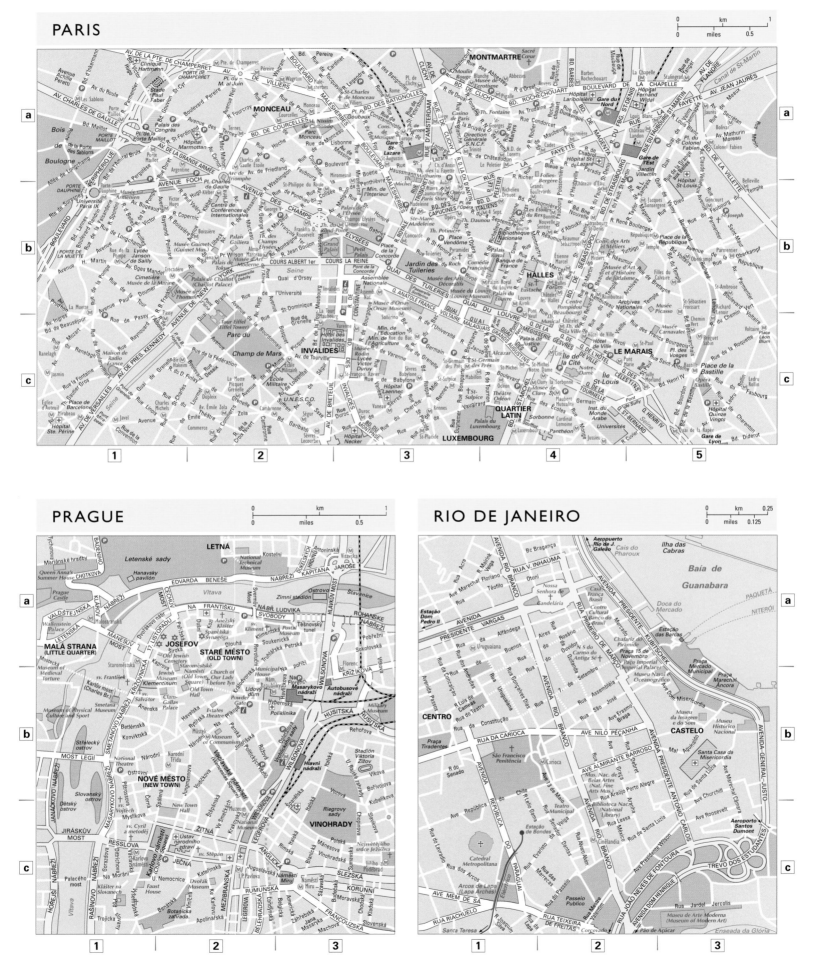

PARIS

PRAGUE

RIO DE JANEIRO

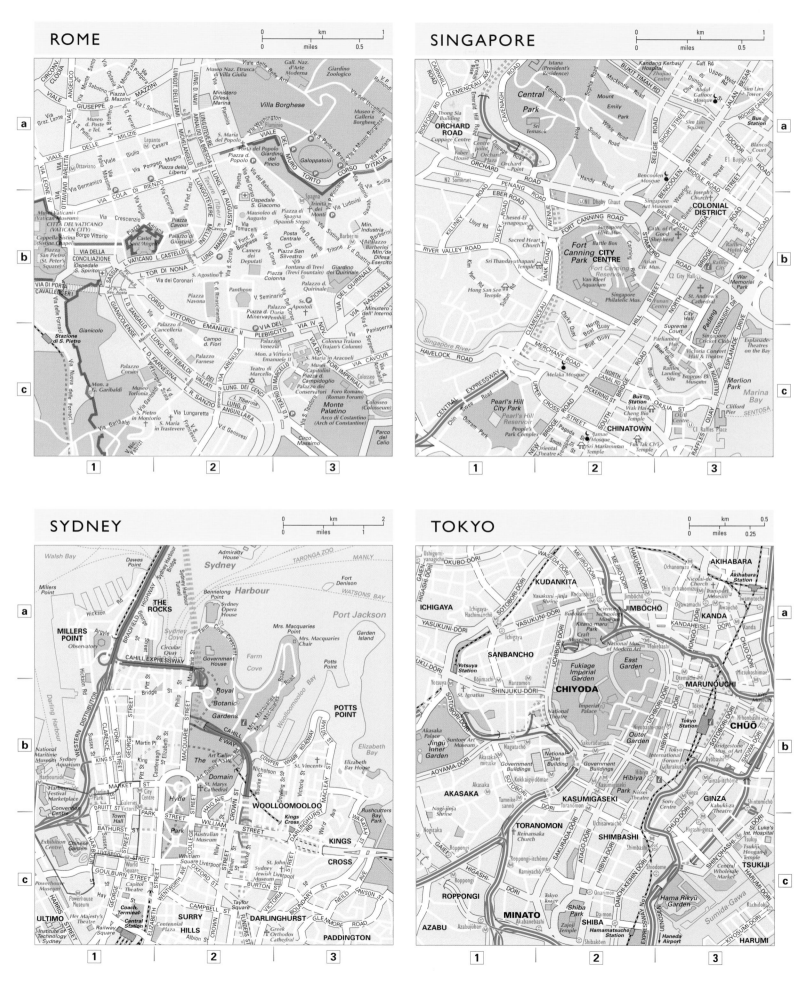

ROME

SINGAPORE

SYDNEY

TOKYO

The table shows air distances in kilometres and miles between 24 major cities. Known as 'great circle' distances, these measure the shortest routes between the cities, which are used by aircraft wherever possible. The maps show the world centred on six cities, and illustrate, for example, why direct flights from Japan to North America and Europe are across the Arctic regions. The maps have been constructed on an Azimuthal Equidistant projection, on which all distances measured through the centre point are true to scale. The red lines are drawn at 5,000, 10,000 and 15,000 km from the central city.

Upper-right half of the table (above the diagonal) gives distances in miles; lower-left half (below the diagonal) gives distances in Kms.

	Beijing	Buenos Aires	Cairo	Caracas	Chicago	Hong Kong	Honolulu	Johannesburg	Kolkata	Lagos	London	Los Angeles	Mexico City	Moscow	Mumbai	Nairobi	New York	Paris	Rio de Janeiro	Rome	Singapore	Sydney	Tokyo	Wellington
Beijing		11972	4688	8947	6588	1220	5070	7276	2031	7119	5057	6251	7742	3600	2956	5727	6828	5106	10773	5049	2783	5561	1304	6700
Buenos Aires	19268		7341	3167	5599	11481	7558	5025	10268	4919	6917	6122	4591	8374	9275	6463	5298	6867	1214	6929	9867	7332	11410	6202
Cairo	7544	11814		6340	6127	5064	8838	3894	3541	2432	2180	7580	7687	1803	2706	2197	5605	1994	6149	1325	5137	8959	5947	10268
Caracas	14399	5096	10203		2502	10166	6009	6847	9609	4810	4664	3612	2228	6175	9024	7173	2131	4738	2825	5196	11407	9534	8801	8154
Chicago	10603	9011	3206	4027		7783	4247	8689	7978	5973	3949	1742	1694	4971	8048	8005	711	4132	5311	4809	9369	9243	6299	8358
Hong Kong	1963	18478	8150	16360	12526		5543	6669	1653	7360	5980	7232	8775	4439	2683	5453	8047	5984	11001	5769	1615	4582	1786	5857
Honolulu	8160	12164	14223	9670	6836	8921		11934	7048	10133	7228	2558	3781	7036	8024	10739	4958	7437	8290	8026	6721	5075	3854	4669
Johannesburg	11710	8088	6267	11019	13984	10732	19206		5256	2799	5637	10362	9063	5692	4334	1818	7979	5426	4420	4811	5381	6860	8418	7308
Kolkata	3269	16524	5699	15464	12839	2659	11343	8459		5727	4946	8152	9494	3438	1034	3839	7921	4883	9366	4486	1800	5678	3195	7055
Lagos	11457	7916	3915	7741	9612	11845	16308	4505	9216		3118	7713	6879	3886	4730	2366	5268	2929	3750	2510	6925	9643	8376	9973
London	8138	11131	3508	7507	6356	9623	11632	9071	7961	5017		5442	5552	1552	4467	4237	3463	212	5778	889	6743	10558	5942	11691
Los Angeles	10060	9852	12200	5812	2804	11639	4117	16676	13120	12414	8758		1549	6070	8700	9659	2446	5645	6310	6331	8776	7502	5475	6719
Mexico City	12460	7389	12372	3586	2726	14122	6085	14585	15280	11071	8936	2493		6664	9728	9207	2090	5717	4780	6365	10321	8058	7024	6897
Moscow	5794	13477	2902	9938	8000	7144	11323	9161	5534	6254	2498	9769	10724		3126	3942	4666	1545	7184	1477	5237	9008	4651	10283
Mumbai	4757	14925	4355	14522	12953	4317	12914	6974	1664	7612	7190	14000	15656	5031		2816	7793	4356	8332	3837	2432	6313	4189	7686
Nairobi	9216	10402	3536	11544	12883	8776	17282	2927	6179	3807	6819	15544	14818	6344	4532		7358	4029	5548	3350	4635	7552	6996	8490
New York	10988	8526	9020	3430	1145	12950	7980	12841	12747	8477	5572	3936	3264	7510	12541	11842		3626	4832	4280	9531	9935	6741	8951
Paris	8217	11051	3210	7625	6650	9630	11968	8732	7858	4714	342	9085	9200	2486	7010	6485	5836		5708	687	6671	10539	6038	11798
Rio de Janeiro	17338	1953	9896	4546	8547	17704	13342	7113	15073	6035	9299	10155	7693	11562	13409	8928	7777	9187		5725	9763	8389	11551	7367
Rome	8126	11151	2133	8363	7739	9284	12916	7743	7219	4039	1431	10188	10243	2376	6175	5391	6888	1105	9214		6229	10143	6127	11523
Singapore	4478	15879	8267	18359	15078	2599	10816	8660	2897	11145	10852	14123	16610	8428	3914	7460	15339	10737	15712	10025		3915	3306	5298
Sydney	8949	11800	14418	15343	14875	7374	8168	11040	9138	15519	16992	12073	12969	14497	10160	12153	15989	16962	13501	16324	6300		4861	1383
Tokyo	2099	18362	9571	14164	10137	2874	6202	13547	5141	13480	9562	8811	11304	7485	6742	11260	10849	9718	18589	9861	5321	7823		5762
Wellington	10782	9981	16524	13122	13451	9427	7513	11761	11354	16050	18814	10814	11100	16549	12370	13664	14405	18987	11855	18545	8526	2226	9273	

MEXICO CITY
19° 26'N 99° 04'W

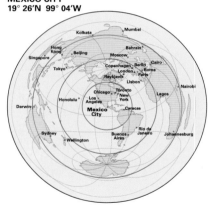

LONDON
51° 28'N 00° 27'W

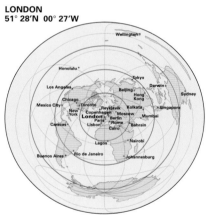

TOKYO
35° 33'N 139° 46'E

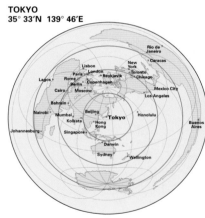

RIO DE JANEIRO
22° 50'S 43° 15'W

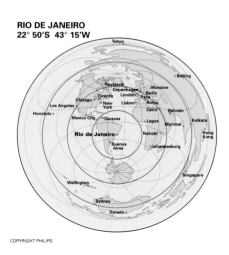

SINGAPORE
1° 21'N 103° 54'E

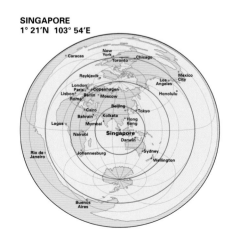

SYDNEY
33° 56' S 151° 10'E

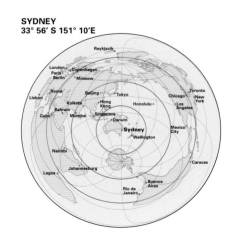

WORLD MAPS

SETTLEMENTS

■ PARIS   ■ Berne   ◉ Livorno   ◉ Brugge   ◎ Algeciras   ○ Frejus   ○ Oberammergau   ○ Thira

Settlement symbols and type styles vary according to the scale of each map and indicate the importance
of towns on the map rather than specific population figures. Capital cities have red infills.

ADMINISTRATION

——— International boundaries

– – – International boundaries
(undefined or disputed)

·············· Internal boundaries

·---------- National park boundaries

International boundaries show the *de facto* situation where there are rival claims to territory

COMMUNICATIONS

——— Principal roads

——— Principal railways

+–·–+ Railway tunnels

+–·–+ Road tunnels

–·–·– Railways
under construction

⊞⊞⊞⊞ Principal canals

⤫ Passes

⊕ Airfields

PHYSICAL FEATURES

〜〜 Perennial streams

⬭ Intermittent lakes

▲ 8848 Elevations in metres

–·–· Intermittent streams

⬭ Swamps and marshes

▼ 8500 Sea depths in metres

◯ Perennial lakes

❄ Permanent ice
and glaciers

1134 Height of lake surface
above sea level in metres

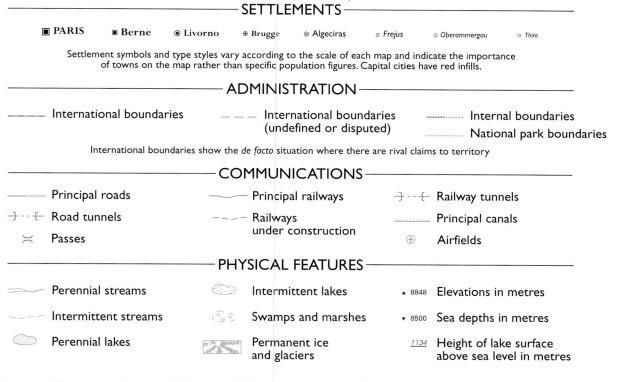

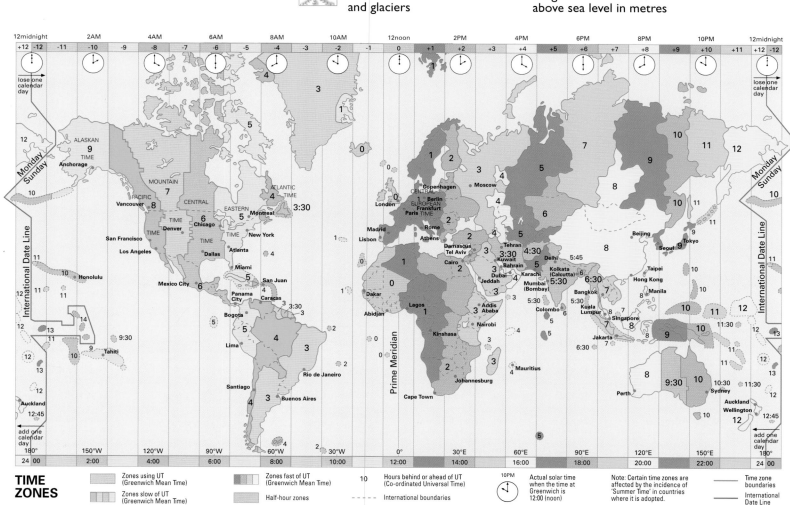

**TIME
ZONES**

Zones using UT
(Greenwich Mean Time)

Zones slow of UT
(Greenwich Mean Time)

Zones fast of UT
(Greenwich Mean Time)

Half-hour zones

10 Hours behind or ahead of UT
(Co-ordinated Universal Time)

– – – International boundaries

10PM
🕙 Actual solar time
when the time at
Greenwich is
12:00 (noon)

Note: Certain time zones are
affected by the incidence of
'Summer Time' in countries
where it is adopted.

——— Time zone
boundaries

——— International
Date Line

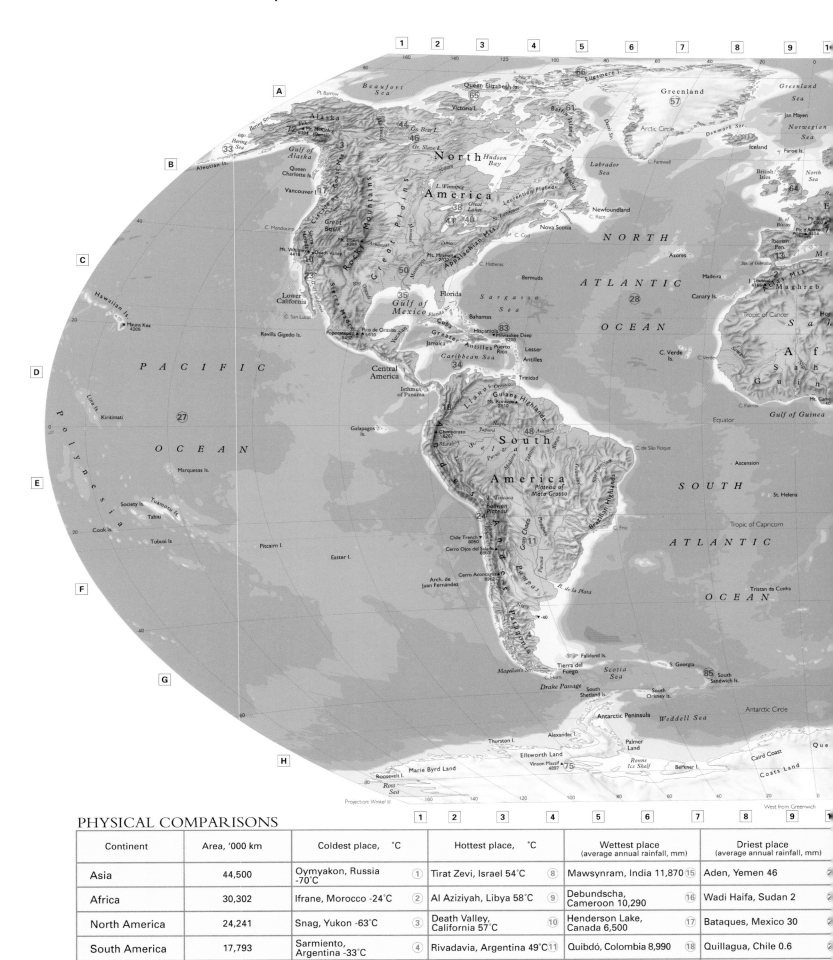

PHYSICAL COMPARISONS

Continent	Area, '000 km	Coldest place, °C	Hottest place, °C	Wettest place (average annual rainfall, mm)	Driest place (average annual rainfall, mm)
Asia	44,500	Oymyakon, Russia -70°C ①	Tirat Zevi, Israel 54°C ⑧	Mawsynram, India 11,870 ⑮	Aden, Yemen 46
Africa	30,302	Ifrane, Morocco -24°C ②	Al Aziziyah, Libya 58°C ⑨	Debundscha, Cameroon 10,290 ⑯	Wadi Haifa, Sudan 2
North America	24,241	Snag, Yukon -63°C ③	Death Valley, California 57°C ⑩	Henderson Lake, Canada 6,500 ⑰	Bataques, Mexico 30
South America	17,793	Sarmiento, Argentina -33°C ④	Rivadavia, Argentina 49°C⑪	Quibdó, Colombia 8,990 ⑱	Quillagua, Chile 0.6
Antarctica	14,000	Vostok -89°C ⑤	Vanda Station 15°C ⑫		
Europe	9,957	Ust'Shchugor, Russia -55°C ⑥	Seville, Spain 50°C ⑬	Crkvice, Serbia & M. 4,650⑲	Astrakhan, Russia 160
Oceania	8,557	Charlotte Pass, Australia -22°C ⑦	Cloncurry, Australia 53°C ⑭	Tully, Australia 4,550 ⑳	Mulka, Australia 100

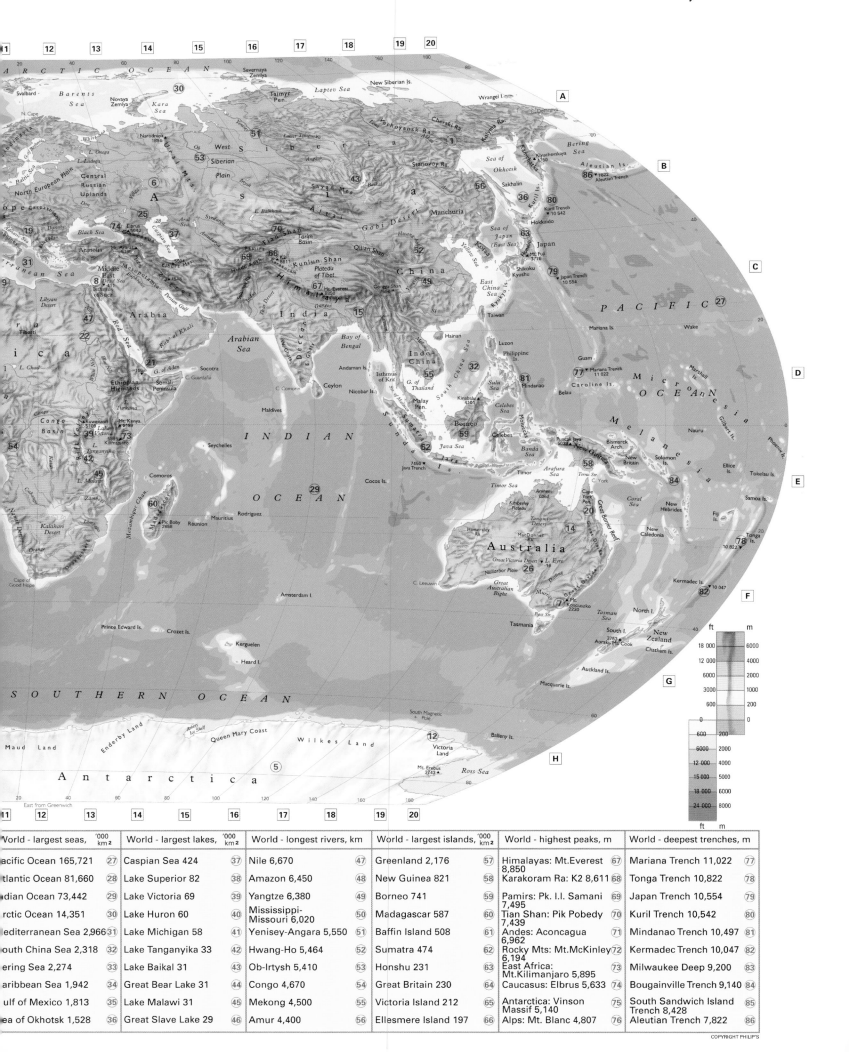

World - largest seas, '000 km²		World - largest lakes, '000 km²		World - longest rivers, km		World - largest islands, '000 km²		World - highest peaks, m		World - deepest trenches, m	
Pacific Ocean 165,721	27	Caspian Sea 424	37	Nile 6,670	47	Greenland 2,176	57	Himalayas: Mt.Everest 8,850	67	Mariana Trench 11,022	77
Atlantic Ocean 81,660	28	Lake Superior 82	38	Amazon 6,450	48	New Guinea 821	58	Karakoram Ra: K2 8,611	68	Tonga Trench 10,822	78
Indian Ocean 73,442	29	Lake Victoria 69	39	Yangtze 6,380	49	Borneo 741	59	Pamirs: Pk. I.I. Samani 7,495	69	Japan Trench 10,554	79
Arctic Ocean 14,351	30	Lake Huron 60	40	Mississippi-Missouri 6,020	50	Madagascar 587	60	Tian Shan: Pik Pobedy 7,439	70	Kuril Trench 10,542	80
Mediterranean Sea 2,966	31	Lake Michigan 58	41	Yenisey-Angara 5,550	51	Baffin Island 508	61	Andes: Aconcagua 6,962	71	Mindanao Trench 10,497	81
South China Sea 2,318	32	Lake Tanganyika 33	42	Hwang-Ho 5,464	52	Sumatra 474	62	Rocky Mts: Mt.McKinley 6,194	72	Kermadec Trench 10,047	82
Bering Sea 2,274	33	Lake Baikal 31	43	Ob-Irtysh 5,410	53	Honshu 231	63	East Africa: Mt.Kilimanjaro 5,895	73	Milwaukee Deep 9,200	83
Caribbean Sea 1,942	34	Great Bear Lake 31	44	Congo 4,670	54	Great Britain 230	64	Caucasus: Elbrus 5,633	74	Bougainville Trench 9,140	84
Gulf of Mexico 1,813	35	Lake Malawi 31	45	Mekong 4,500	55	Victoria Island 212	65	Antarctica: Vinson Massif 5,140	75	South Sandwich Island Trench 8,428	85
Sea of Okhotsk 1,528	36	Great Slave Lake 29	46	Amur 4,400	56	Ellesmere Island 197	66	Alps: Mt. Blanc 4,807	76	Aleutian Trench 7,822	86

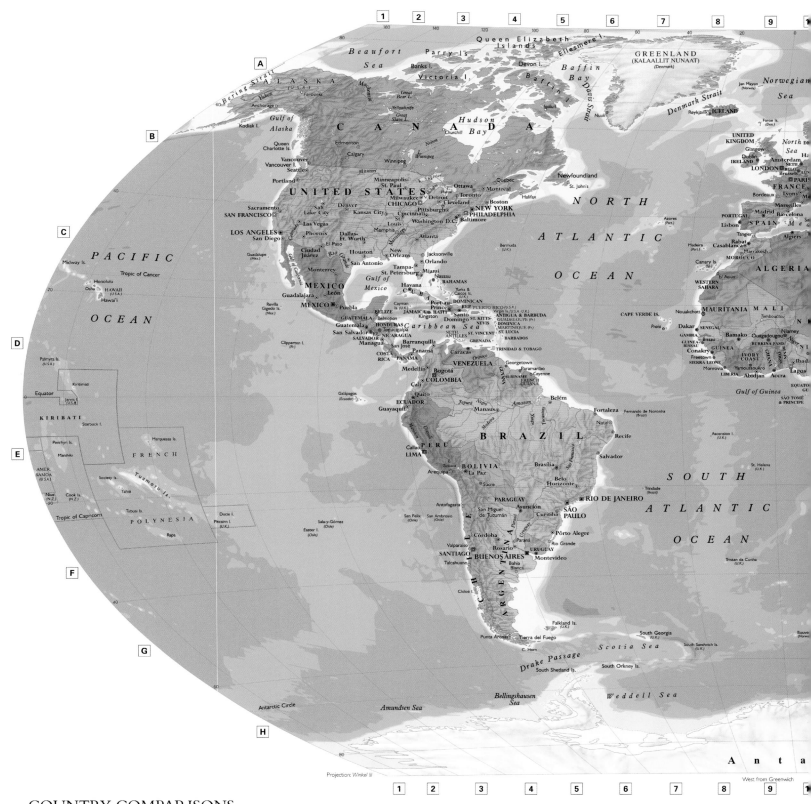

COUNTRY COMPARISONS

Country	Population in thousands 2005 estimate	Area in thous' km²	Country	Population in thousands 2005 estimate	Area in thous' km²	Country	Population in thousands 2005 estimate	Area in thous' km²	Country	Population in thousands 2005 estimate	Area in thous' km²	Country	Population in thousands 2005 estimate	Area in thous' km²
China	1,306,300	9,597	Mexico	106,200	1,958	France	60,700	552	Argentina	39,500	2,780	Uganda	27,300	2
India	1,080,300	3,287	Philippines	87,900	300	United Kingdom	60,400	242	Poland	38,600	323	Uzbekistan	26,900	4
United States	295,700	9,629	Vietnam	83,500	332	Italy	58,100	301	Tanzania	36,800	945	Saudi Arabia	26,400	2,1
Indonesia	242,000	1,905	Germany	82,400	357	South Korea	48,600	99	Kenya	33,800	580	Iraq	26,100	4
Brazil	186,100	8,514	Egypt	77,500	1,001	Ukraine	47,000	604	Canada	32,800	9,971	Venezuela	25,400	9
Pakistan	162,400	796	Ethiopia	73,100	1,104	Burma (Myanmar)	47,000	677	Morocco	32,700	447	Malaysia	24,000	3
Bangladesh	144,300	144	Turkey	69,700	775	South Africa	44,300	1,221	Algeria	32,500	2,382	North Korea	22,900	
Russia	143,400	17,075	Iran	68,000	1,648	Colombia	43,000	1,139	Afghanistan	29,900	652	Taiwan	22,900	
Nigeria	128,800	924	Thailand	64,200	513	Spain	40,300	498	Peru	27,900	1,285	Romania	22,300	2
Japan	127,400	378	Congo, Dem. Rep.	60,800	2,345	Sudan	40,200	2,506	Nepal	27,700	147	Ghana	21,900	2

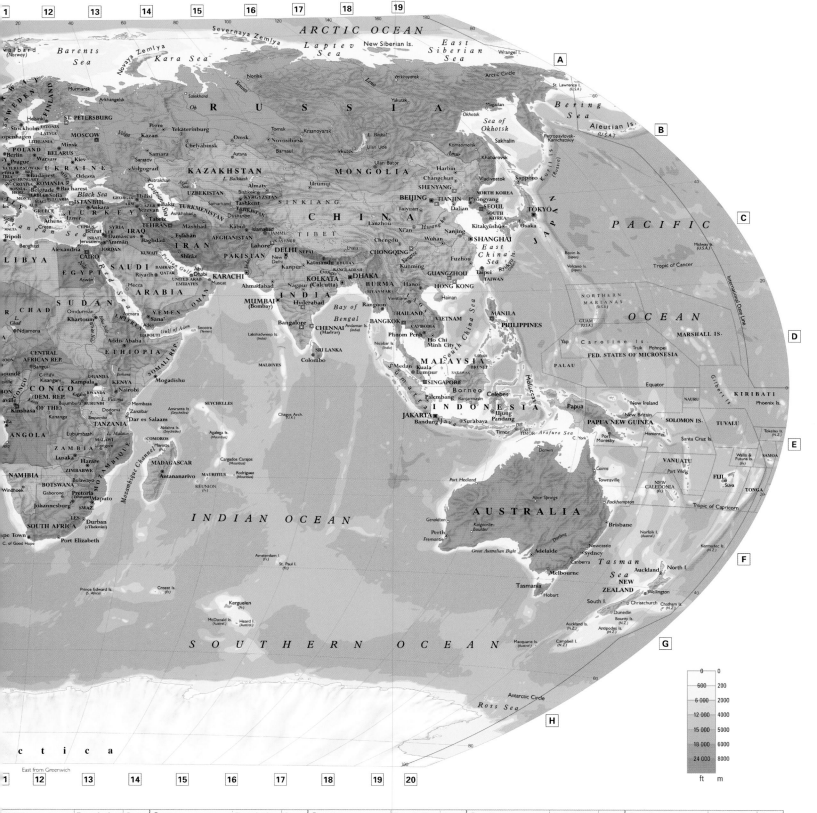

Country	Population in thousands 2005 estimate	Area in thous' km²	Country	Population in thousands 2005 estimate	Area in thous' km²	Country	Population in thousands 2005 estimate	Area in thous' km²	Country	Population in thousands 2005 estimate	Area in thous' km²	Country	Population in thousands 2005 estimate	Area in thous' km²
...emen	20,700	528	Kazakhstan	15,200	2,725	Mali	11,400	1,240	Hungary	10,000	93	Azerbaijan	7,900	87
...ustralia	20,100	7,741	Cambodia	13,600	181	Cuba	11,300	111	Chad	9,700	1,284	Burundi	7,800	28
...i Lanka	20,100	66	Burkina Faso	13,500	274	Zambia	11,300	753	Guinea	9,500	246	Benin	7,600	113
...ozambique	19,400	802	Ecuador	13,400	284	Greece	10,700	132	Dominican Rep.	9,000	49	Switzerland	7,500	41
...yria	18,400	185	Malawi	12,700	118	Portugal	10,600	89	Sweden	9,000	450	Bulgaria	7,500	111
...adagascar	18,000	587	Niger	12,200	1,267	Belgium	10,400	31	Bolivia	8,900	1,099	Honduras	7,200	112
...ory Coast	17,300	322	Zimbabwe	12,200	394	Belarus	10,300	208	Somalia	8,600	638	Tajikistan	7,200	143
...ameroon	17,000	475	Guatemala	12,000	109	Czech Republic	10,200	79	Rwanda	8,400	26	Hong Kong (China)	6,900	1
...etherlands	16,400	42	Angola	11,800	1,247	Tunisia	10,100	164	Austria	8,200	84	El Salvador	6,700	21
...hile	16,000	757	Senegal	11,700	197	Serbia	10,100	88	Haiti	8,100	28	Paraguay	6,300	407

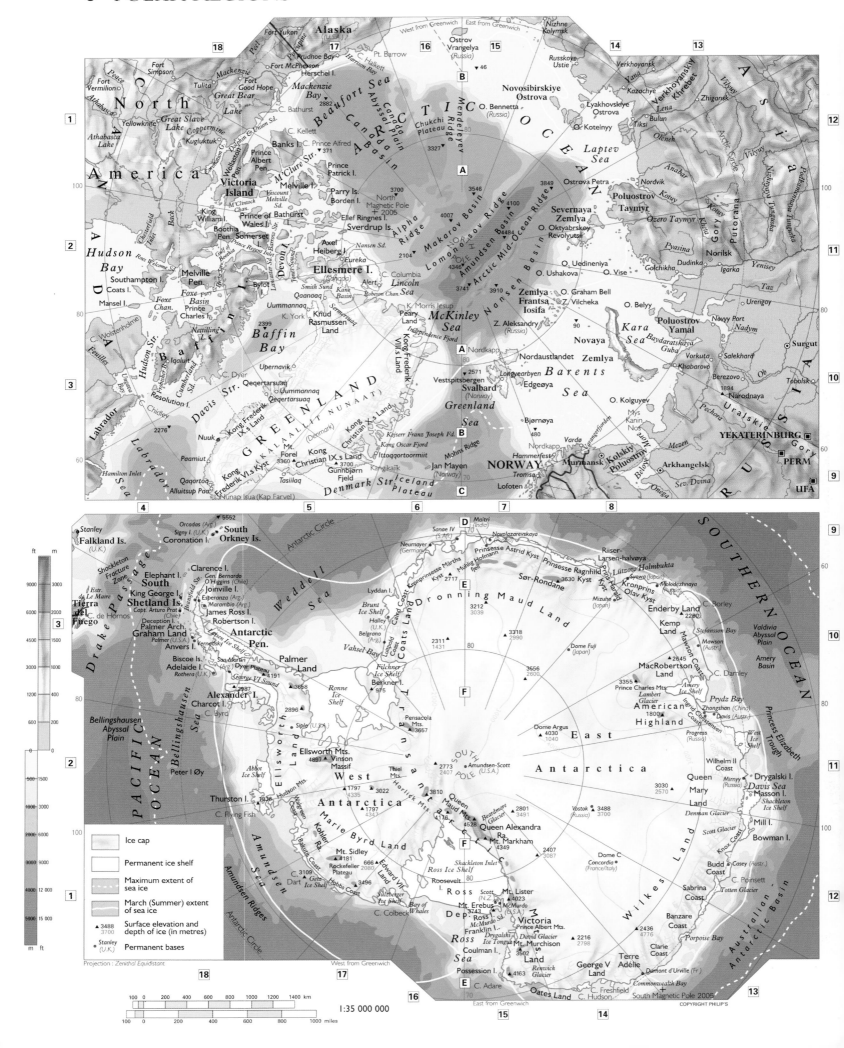

North Polar map labels:

North America · CANADA · Alaska (U.S.A.) · ARCTIC OCEAN · Greenland (KALAALLIT NUNAAT) (Denmark) · ASIA · RUSSIA · NORWAY

Fort Yukon · Fort Simpson · Fort Vermilion · Fort Good Hope · Fort McPherson · Peace · Athabasca · Great Slave Lake · Great Bear Lake · Yellowknife · Coppermine · Kugluktuk · Tulita · Mackenzie · Mackenzie Bay · Herschel I. · Pt. Barrow · Prudhoe Bay · C. Halkett · Harrison Bay · C. Bathurst · 2882 · C. Kellett · Beaufort Sea · Banks I. · C. Prince Alfred · 371 · Prince Patrick I. · M'Clure Str. · Melville I. · Parry Is. · Borden I. · 3700 · Elef Ringnes I. · North Magnetic Pole 2005 · 3327 · Chukchi Plateau · Mendeleyev Ridge · Alpha Ridge · 4007 · Makarov Basin · Lomonosov Ridge · Amundsen Basin · NORTH POLE · 4346 · 3741 · 2104 · 3910 · 4484 · 4100 · Nansen Basin · Arctic Mid-Ocean Ridge · 3849 · 3546 · Canada Basin · Canada Abyssal Plain · Ostrov Vrangelya (Russia) · 46 · Novosibirskiye Ostrova · O. Bennetta (Russia) · Nizhne Kolymsk · Russkoye Ustie · Verkhoyansk · Yana · Kazachye · Lyakhovskiye Ostrova · Lena · Bulun · Tiksi · O. Kotelnyy · Laptev Sea · Olenek · Anabar · Nordvik · Khatanga · Ostrova Petra · Poluostrov Taymyr · Severnaya Zemlya · Oktyabrskey Revolyutsii · O. Uedineniya · O. Ushakova · Z. Vilcheka · Zemlya Frantsa Iosifa · O. Graham Bell · Z. Aleksandry (Russia) · 90 · Kara Sea · Poluostrov Yamal · Novaya Zemlya · Barents Sea

Great Slave Lake · Athabasca Lake · Coppermine · Chesterfield Inlet · Victoria Island · Wollaston Pen. · Prince Albert Pen. · Melville Pen. · M'Clintock Chan. · Prince of Wales I. · King William I. · Boothia Pen. · Somerset I. · Devon I. · Prince of Bathurst · Viscount Melville Sd. · Sverdrup Is. · Axel Heiberg I. · Nansen Sd. · Eureka · Ellesmere I. (Canada) · Alert · C. Columbia · Lincoln Sea · Robeson Chan. · Kane Basin · Smith Sund · Peary Land · Independence Fjord · Kong Frederik VIII's Land · McKinley Sea · Nordkapp · Nordaustlandet · Zemlya · Novaya Zemlya

Hudson Bay · Southampton I. · Coats I. · Mansel I. · Roes Welcome Sd. · Foxe Basin · Foxe Chan. · Prince Charles I. · Baffin I. (Canada) · 2399 · Bylot · K. York · K. Morris Jesup · Knud Rasmussen Land · Qaanaaq · Uummannaq · Baydaratskaya Guba · Vorkuta · Khabarovo · Salekhard · 1894 · Narodnaya · Berezovo · Ob · Surgut · Tobolsk · YEKATERINBURG · PERM · UFA

Labrador · Hudson Str. · Ungava Bay · Davis Str. · C. Dyer · Iqaluit · Cumberland Sd. · Resolution I. · Chidley · 2276 · Qeqertarsuaq · Uummannaq · Qeqertarsuaq · Upernavik · Nuuk · Paamiut · GREENLAND · Kong Frederik IX's Land · Mt. Forel · 3360 · Kong Christian IX's Land · Kong Christian X's Land · Kong Frederik VI's Land · Gunnbjørn Fjeld · 3700 · Tasiilaq · Ittoqqortoormiit · Kong Oscar Fjord · Kejser Franz Joseph Fd. · Nunap Isua (Kap Farvel) · Qaqortoq · Alluitsup Paa · Denmark Str. · Iceland Plateau · Kangikajik · Scoresbysund · Greenland Sea · Mohns Ridge · Jan Mayen (Norway) · Vestspitsbergen · Svalbard (Norway) · 2571 · Edgeøya · Longyearbyen · Bjørnøya · 480 · Nordkapp · Hammerfest · Tromsø · Murmansk · Kolskiy Poluostrov · Arkhangelsk · Vardø · Mys Kanin Nos · Mezen · Onega · Sev. Dvina · Pechora · Belaya

South Polar map labels:

SOUTHERN OCEAN · PACIFIC OCEAN · Antarctica · East Antarctica · West Antarctica

Stanley · Falkland Is. (U.K.) · Orcadas (Arg.) · 5552 · Signy I. (U.K.) · South Orkney Is. · Coronation I. · Antarctic Circle · Maitri (India) · Sanae IV (S. Afr.) · Novolazarevskaya · Neumayer (Germany) · Prinsesse Astrid Kyst · Prinsesse Ragnhild Kyst · Riiser-Larsen-halvøya · Lützow Holmbukta · Syowa (Japan) · Molodezhnaya · Kronprins Olav Kyst · Enderby Land · C. Borley

Tierra del Fuego · C. de Hornos · Estr. de Le Maire · Drake Passage · Shackleton Fracture Zone · Elephant I. · Clarence I. · King George I. · Joinville I. · South Shetland Is. · Gen. Bernardo O'Higgins (Chile) · Esperanza (Arg.) · Marambio (Arg.) · Capt. Arturo Prat (Chile) · Bransfield Str. · James Ross I. · Robertson I. · Deception I. · Palmer Arch. · Graham Land · Palmer (U.S.A.) · Anvers I. · Vernadsky · Biscoe Is. · Adelaide I. · Rothera (U.K.) · San Martín (Arg.) · Dyer Plateau · George VI Sound · 191 · Alexander I. · 2987 · 3658 · Charcot I. · C. Byrd · 2896 · Siple (U.S.A.)

Weddell Sea · Lyddan I. · Brunt Ice Shelf · Halley (U.K.) · Belgrano (Arg.) · Vahsel Bay · Filchner Ice Shelf · Berkner I. · 975 · Ronne Ice Shelf · Luitpold Coast · Coats Land · Caird Coast · Comprinsesse Martha Kyst · Mühlig Hofmann fjell · 2717 · Dronning Maud Land · 3212 · 3039 · 2311 · 1431 · 3318 · 2990 · 3556 · 2600 · 3355 · 3630 · Sør-Rondane · Mizuho (Japan) · Mawson (Austr.) · 2645 · Kemp Land · MacRobertson Land · 2280 · Stefansson Bay · Valdivia Abyssal Plain · Amery Basin · C. Darnley · Prince Charles Mts. · Amery Ice Shelf · Lambert Glacier · Prydz Bay · Zhongshan (China) · Davis (Austr.) · American Highland · Ingrid Christensen Coast · West Ice Shelf · Princess Elizabeth Trough

Bellingshausen Abyssal Plain · Bellingshausen Sea · Peter I Øy · Thurston I. · 1038 · C. Flying Fish · Ellsworth Land · Abbot Ice Shelf · Hudson Mts. · 1797 · 4335 · 3022 · Ellsworth Mts. · 4897 · Vinson Massif · West Antarctica · Thiel Mts. · 2773 · 2407 · SOUTH POLE · Amundsen-Scott (U.S.A.) · Dome Fuji (Japan) · 4030 · 1040 · Dome Argus · Vostok (Russia) · 3488 · 3700 · East Antarctica · Progress (Russia) · Wilhelm II Land · Queen Mary Land · 3030 · 2570 · Mirnyy (Russia) · Drygalski I. · Davis Sea · Masson I. · Shackleton Ice Shelf · Bowman I.

Amundsen Sea · Amundsen Ridges · Marie Byrd Land · Kohler Ra. · Bakutis Coast · Walgreen Coast · 1797 · 4341 · 3810 · 4116 · Transantarctic Mts. · Horlick Mts. · Queen Maud Mts. · 4528 · Beardmore Glacier · 2801 · 3491 · Queen Alexandra Ra. · Mt. Markham · 4349 · 2407 · 3087 · Dome C · Concordia (France/Italy) · Mt. Sidley · 4181 · 666 · 2080 · Rockefeller Plateau · Edward VII Land · 3109 · Dart · Getz Ice Shelf · 3496 · Gobbs Coast · Sulzberger Ice Shelf · Roosevelt I. · Shackleton Inlet · Ross Ice Shelf · Bay of Whales · Ross Sea · Scott (N.Z.) · McMurdo (U.S.A.) · Mt. Lister · 4023 · Mt. Erebus · 3743 · Ross I. · McMurdo Sd. · Franklin I. · Victoria Land · Prince Albert Mts. · Drygalski Ice Tongue · David Glacier · 2216 · 2798 · Mt. Murchison · 3502 · Coulman I. · 4163 · Renwick Glacier · Possession I. · C. Adare · Oates Land · C. Freshfield · George V Land · C. Hudson · Terre Adélie · Dumont d'Urville (Fr.) · Commonwealth Bay · South Magnetic Pole 2005 · Scott Glacier · Knox Coast · Budd Coast · Casey (Austr.) · Sabrina Coast · Totten Glacier · Banzare Coast · Clarie Coast · Porpoise Bay · Wilkes Land · Denman Glacier · Mill I. · 2436 · 4776 · Knox Coast · Australian Antarctic Basin

West from Greenwich · East from Greenwich · Antarctic Circle

Legend / Scale:

ft · m · 9000 / 3000 · 6000 / 2000 · 4500 / 1500 · 3000 / 1000 · 1200 / 400 · 600 / 200 · 0 / 0 · 500 / 1500 · 1000 / 3000 · 2000 / 6000 · 3000 / 9000 · 4000 / 12 000 · 5000 / 15 000 · m · ft

Symbol	Description
	Ice cap
	Permanent ice shelf
	Maximum extent of sea ice
	March (Summer) extent of sea ice
▲ 3488 / 3700	Surface elevation and depth of ice (in metres)
• Stanley (U.K.)	Permanent bases

Projection : Zenithal Equidistant

100 · 0 · 200 · 400 · 600 · 800 · 1000 · 1200 · 1400 km
100 · 0 · 200 · 400 · 600 · 800 · 1000 miles

1:35 000 000

1:10 000 000

Projection: Conical with two standard parallels

East from Greenwich

COPYRIGHT PHILIP'S

10 0 10 20 30 40 50 60 70 80 km
10 0 10 20 30 40 50 miles

1:2 000 000

Key to English unitary authorities on map

25 HARTLEPOOL
26 DARLINGTON
27 STOCKTON-ON-TEES
28 MIDDLESBROUGH
29 REDCAR AND CLEVELAND
30 BLACKPOOL
31 BLACKBURN WITH DARWEN
32 HALTON
33 WARRINGTON
34 KINGSTON UPON HULL
35 NORTH EAST LINCOLNSHIRE
36 STOKE-ON-TRENT
37 TELFORD AND WREKIN
38 DERBY CITY
39 CITY OF NOTTINGHAM
40 LEICESTER CITY
41 RUTLAND
42 PETERBOROUGH
43 MILTON KEYNES
44 LUTON
45 NORTH SOMERSET
46 CITY OF BRISTOL
47 BATH AND NORTH EAST SOMERSET
48 SWINDON
49 READING
50 WOKINGHAM
51 WINDSOR AND MAIDENHEAD
52 SLOUGH
53 BRACKNELL FOREST
54 THURROCK
55 SOUTHEND-ON-SEA
56 MEDWAY
57 PLYMOUTH
58 TORBAY
59 POOLE
60 BOURNEMOUTH
61 SOUTHAMPTON
62 PORTSMOUTH
63 BRIGHTON AND HOVE

Key to Welsh unitary authorities on map

15 SWANSEA
16 NEATH PORT TALBOT
17 BRIDGEND
18 RHONDDA CYNON TAFF
19 MERTHYR TYDFIL
20 CAERPHILLY
21 BLAENAU GWENT
22 TORFAEN
23 CARDIFF
24 NEWPORT

N O R T H   S E A

I R I S H   S E A

North Channel

NORTHERN IRELAND

SCOTLAND

ENGLAND

GWYNEDD

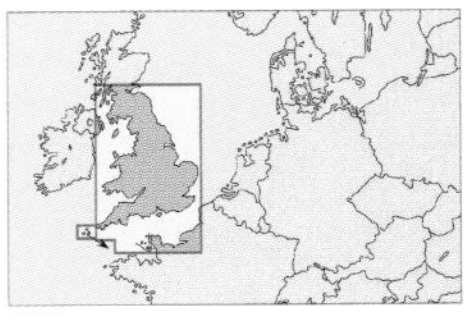

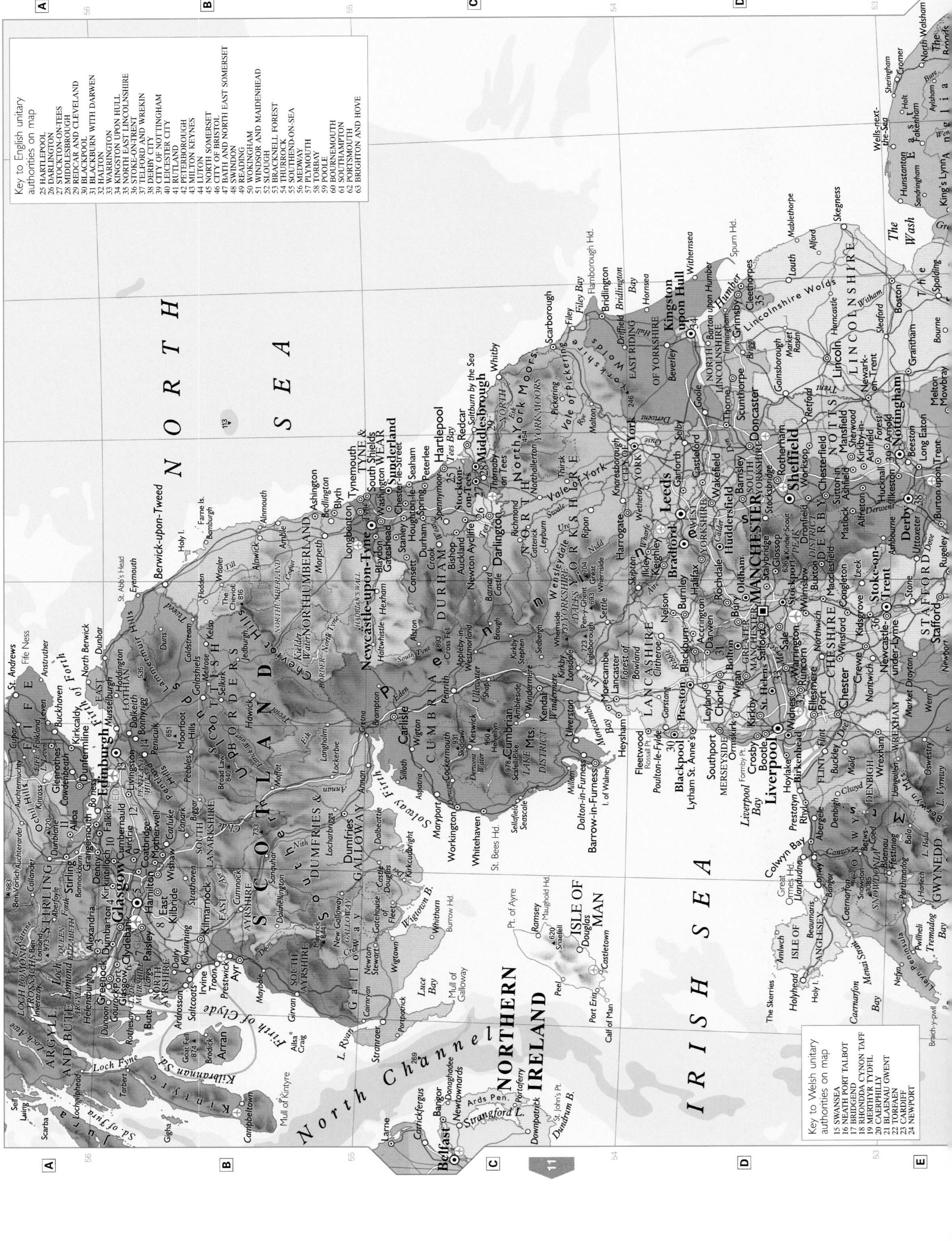

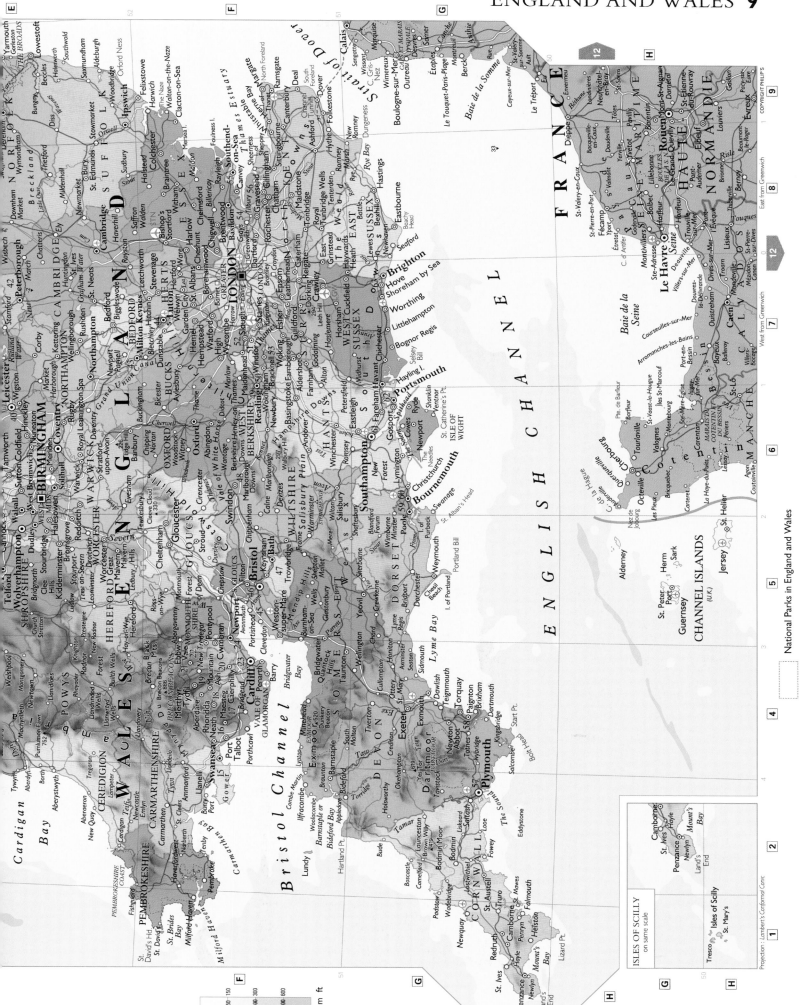

National Parks in England and Wales

ISLES OF SCILLY
on same scale

Projection: Lambert's Conformal Conic

10 SCOTLAND

1:2 000 000

Key to Scottish unitary authorities on map
1 CITY OF ABERDEEN
2 DUNDEE CITY
3 WEST DUNBARTONSHIRE
4 EAST DUNBARTONSHIRE
5 CITY OF GLASGOW
6 INVERCLYDE
7 RENFREWSHIRE
8 EAST RENFREWSHIRE
9 NORTH LANARKSHIRE
10 FALKIRK
11 CLACKMANNANSHIRE
12 WEST LOTHIAN
13 CITY OF EDINBURGH
14 MIDLOTHIAN

ORKNEY IS. on same scale

SHETLAND IS. on same scale

Projection : Lambert's Conformal Conic

West from Greenwich

COPYRIGHT PHILIP'S

National Parks and Forest Parks in Scotland

SCOTLAND · ENGLAND · NORTHERN IRELAND
ATLANTIC OCEAN · NORTH SEA · North Channel
WESTERN ISLES · Lewis · Harris · North Uist · South Uist · Barra
Skye · Mull · Islay · Jura · Arran
HIGHLAND · Inverness · Loch Ness · Ben Nevis · Fort William
Aberdeen · Dundee · Perth · Stirling · Glasgow · Edinburgh
ORKNEY · Kirkwall · SHETLAND · Lerwick · Belfast

National Parks

1:5 000 000

50 0 25 50 75 100 125 150 175 km
50 0 25 50 75 100 125 miles

Corse (Corsica)

COPYRIGHT PHILIP'S

UNITED KINGDOM

GERMANY

BELGIUM

LUXEMBOURG

SWITZERLAND

AUSTRIA

ITALY

ANDORRA

SPAIN

FRANCE

English Channel

Bay of Biscay

MEDITERRANEAN SEA

Golfe du Lion

Golfe de Gascogne

PARIS

MARSEILLE

LYON

MONACO

Brest

Bordeaux

Toulouse

Nantes

Strasbourg

Nancy

Metz

Reims

Rouen

Le Havre

Caen

Rennes

Orléans

Tours

Dijon

Besançon

Clermont-Ferrand

Limoges

Nice

Toulon

Montpellier

Nîmes

Perpignan

Bayonne

Biarritz

Grenoble

St-Étienne

Bern

Zürich

Basel

Genève

Milano

Torino

Genova

Frankfurt

Stuttgart

Karlsruhe

Bonn

Brussel / Bruxelles

Bilbao

Pamplona

Normandie

Bretagne

Aquitaine

Pyrénées

Alpes

Massif Central

Jura

Vosges

Lorraine

Champagne

Île de France

Picardie

Côte d'Azur

Projection: Conical with two standard parallels

m ft
0
50 150
100 300
200 600
500 1500
1000 3000
2000 6000
3000 9000
4000 12000

National Parks

West from Greenwich   East from Greenwich

1:5 000 000

National Parks

National Parks

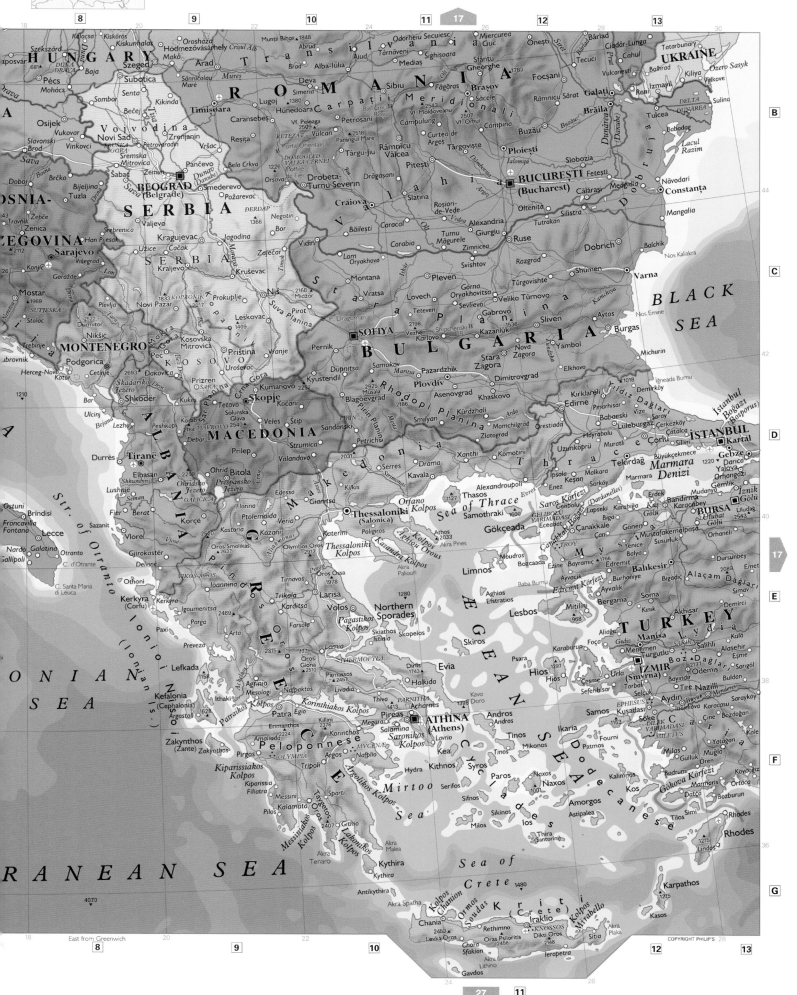

1:5 000 000

50 0 25 50 75 100 125 150 175 km
50 0 25 50 75 100 125 miles

COPYRIGHT PHILIPS

East from Greenwich

Projection: Conical with two standard parallels

Countries and major regions:
RUSSIA · POLAND · GERMANY · CZECH REP. · SLOVAK REP. · HUNGARY · AUSTRIA · SWITZERLAND · FRANCE · BELGIUM · NETHERLANDS · LUXEMBOURG · ITALY · SLOVENIA · CROATIA

Seas:
BALTIC SEA · NORTH SEA

Major cities:
WARSZAWA (Warsaw) · BERLIN · HAMBURG · PRAHA (Prague) · WIEN (Vienna) · BUDAPEST · MÜNCHEN (Munich) · BRATISLAVA · ZAGREB · LJUBLJANA · AMSTERDAM · ROTTERDAM · 's-Gravenhage (Den Haag) · BRUSSEL (Bruxelles) · LUXEMBOURG · LYON

Selected place names:
Kaliningrad · Gdańsk · Gdynia · GSlupsk · Koszalin · Szczecin · Bydgoszcz · Toruń · Poznań · Łódź · Kraków · Katowice · Wrocław · Opole · Kielce · Radom · Lublin · Rostock · Kiel · Lübeck · Schwerin · Bremen · Hannover · Braunschweig · Magdeburg · Leipzig · Dresden · Chemnitz · Erfurt · Frankfurt · Köln · Bonn · Düsseldorf · Dortmund · Essen · Duisburg · Münster · Stuttgart · Mannheim · Karlsruhe · Nürnberg · Augsburg · Regensburg · Salzburg · Linz · Graz · Plzeň · Brno · Ostrava · Olomouc · Zürich · Bern · Basel · Genève · Strasbourg · Nancy · Metz · Dijon · Groningen · Utrecht · Antwerpen · Gent · Maastricht · Liège · Namur · Charleroi · Pécs · Szeged · Győr · Miskolc

BALTIC SEA · NORTH SEA · Zatoka Gdańska · Deutsche Bucht · IJsselmeer

1:10 000 000

50 0 100 200 300 400 km
50 0 50 100 150 200 250 miles

CASPIAN SEA

BLACK SEA

MEDITERRANEAN SEA

ÆGEAN SEA

Sea of Azov

Caucasus Mountains

RUSSIA

UKRAINE
MOLDOVA
ROMANIA
BULGARIA
SERBIA
MACEDONIA
ALBANIA
GREECE
HUNGARY
MONTENEGRO

TURKEY
GEORGIA
ARMENIA
AZERBAIJAN
IRAN
IRAQ (Mesopotamia)
SYRIA
LEBANON
ISRAEL
JORDAN
SAUDI ARABIA
CYPRUS
EGYPT
LIBYA

KALMYKIA
DAGESTAN
CHECHENIA
INGUSHETIA
NORTH OSSETIA
KABARDINO-BALKARIA
KARACHEY-CHERKESSIA
ADYGEYA
ABKHAZIA
AJARIA

Astrakhan
Makhachkala
Grozny
Vladikavkaz
TBILISI
YEREVAN
BAKI (Baku)
TABRĪZ
AL MAWSIL (Mosul)
BAGHDAD
DIMASHQ (Damascus)
BAYRŪT (Beirut)
AMMAN
Jerusalem
TEL AVIV-YAFO
EL QÂHIRA (Cairo)
EL ISKANDARÎYA (Alexandria)
ANKARA
ISTANBUL
İZMIR (Smyrna)
BURSA
ADANA
HALAB (Aleppo)
Hamâh
Hims
BUCUREŞTI (Bucharest)
SOFIA
BEOGRAD
Skopje
Tirana
Athína (Athens)
Thessaloníki
ROSTOV
DONETSK
ODESA
CRIMEA

Kriti (Crete)
Rhodes (Greece)
Dodekánisa
Kykládes / Cyclades
Ioníoi Nísoi
Peloponnese
Pindos Oros

East from Greenwich

Projection: Conical with two standard parallels

m ft
0
-200 - 600
-500 - 1500
1000 - 3000
2000 - 6000
4000 - 12 000

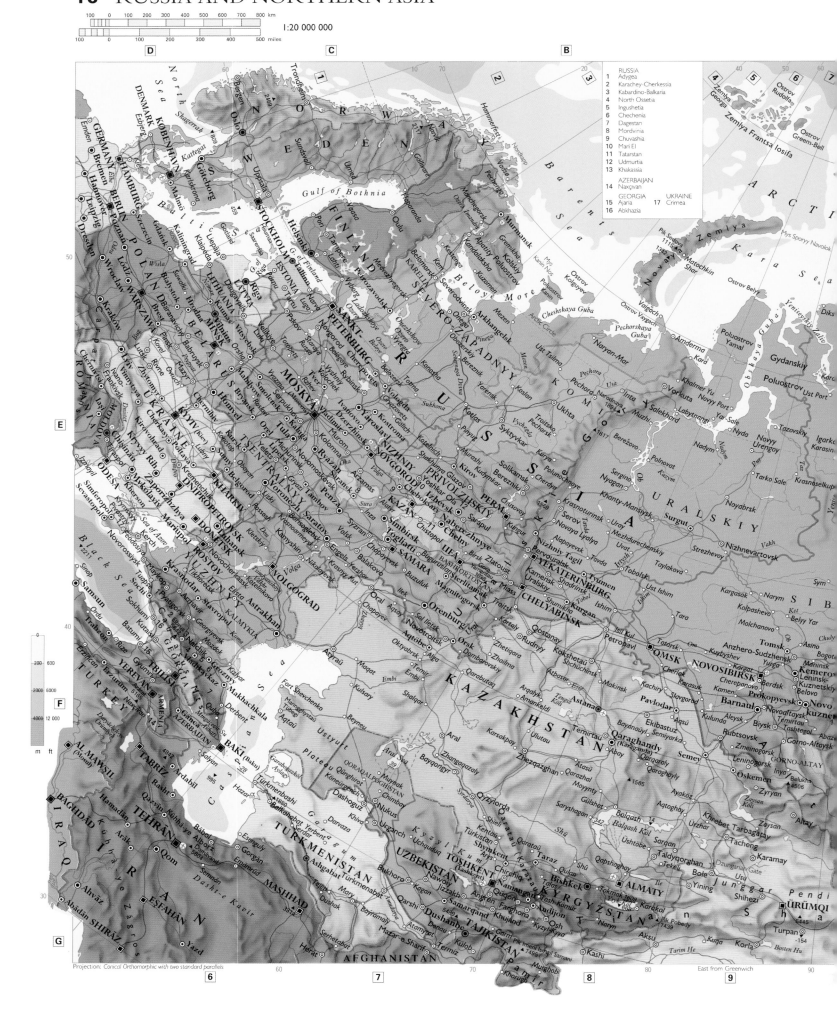

100 0 100 200 300 400 500 600 700 800 km

1:20 000 000

100 0 100 200 300 400 500 miles

RUSSIA
1 Adygea
2 Karachey-Cherkessia
3 Kabardino-Balkaria
4 North Ossetia
5 Ingushetia
6 Chechenia
7 Dagestan
8 Mordvinia
9 Chuvashia
10 Mari El
11 Tatarstan
12 Udmurtia
13 Khakassia

AZERBAIJAN
14 Naxçivan

GEORGIA   UKRAINE
15 Ajaria   17 Crimea
16 Abkhazia

Projection: Conical Orthomorphic with two standard parallels

East from Greenwich

1:15 000 000

Projection: *Bonne*

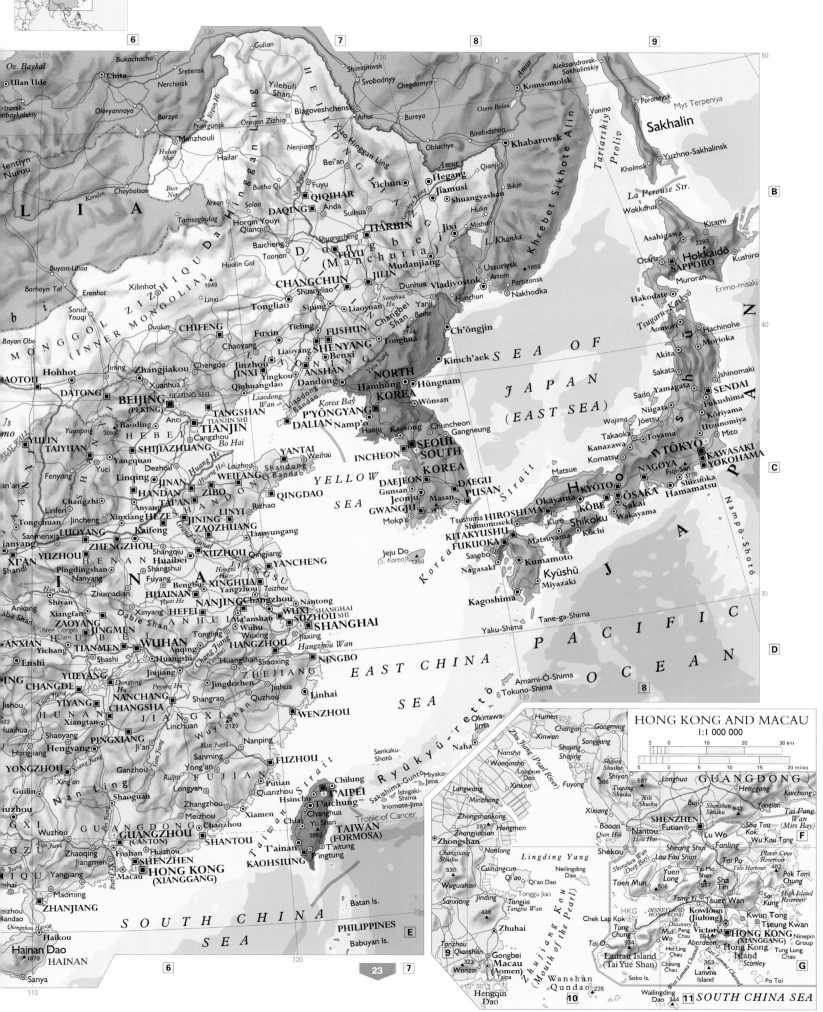

Oz. Baykal
Ulan Ude
Chita
Sretensk
-trovsk-
abaykalskiy
Nerchinsk
Olovyannaya
Borzya
Priargunsk
Shimanovsk
Svobodnyy
Chegdomyn
Komsomolsk
Poronaysk
Mys Terpeniya

Sakhalin

Hentiyn
Nuruu
Kerulen
Choybalsan
Manzhouli
Hailar
Hulun Nur
Bukachacha
Yilehuli Shan
Gulian
Blagoveshchensk
Aihui
Bureya
Ozero Bolon
Birobidzhan
Khabarovsk
Vanino
Kholmsk
Yuzhno-Sakhalinsk
La Perouse Str.
Wakkanai
Kitami
B

Buyant-Uhaa
Borhoyn Tal
Tamsagbulag
Horqin Youyi Qianqi
Solon
Arxan
Butha Qi
Fuyu
QIQIHAR
Anda
DAQING
Qianjin
Yichun
Hegang
Jiamusi
Shuangyashan
Hulin
Mishan
Bikin
Ussuriysk
Artem
1855
Asahigawa
2290
HOKKAIDO
SAPPORO
Otaru
Muroran
Hakodate
Kushiro
Erimo-misaki

Bayan Obo
AOTOU
Hohhot
Jining
Xilinhot
1949
Linxi
Baicheng
Taonan
Shuangcheng
HARBIN
Jixi
Khanka
L. Khanka
Mudanjiang
Vladivostok
Nakhodka
Hunchun
Ch'ongjin
SEA OF
Aomori
Hachinohe
Morioka
Akita

(INNER MONGOLIA)
MONGGOL ZIZHIQU
Erenhot
Sonid Youqi
Duolun
CHIFENG
Chaoyang
Fuxin
Tieling
FUSHUN
SHENYANG
Benxi
JILIN
CHANGCHUN
Siping
Liaoyuan
Tonghua
Tonghua
Changbai Shan
2744
Yanji
Baihe
Kimch'aek
JAPAN
(EAST SEA)
Sakata
Yamagata
Ishinomaki
SENDAI
Fukushima
Koriyama

1:6 400 000

50   0   25   50   75   100   125   150   175 km
50   0   25   50   75   100   125 miles

8
9

CHINA

Jixi
Linkou Novokachalinsk
Kamen-Rybolov
L. Khanka
Suifenhe
Lipovcy
Manzovka
Lesozavodsk
Rakitnoye
Kirovskiy Ariadnoye
Yakovleyka
Arseney
Spassk Dalniy Gornyy
Ussuriysk
Terney
Plastun
Dalnegorsk
Kavalerovo
Margaritovo
Lazo
RUSSIA
Khrebet Sikhote Alin
1855
1498
Hunchun
Slavyanka
Zaliv Petra Velikogo
Khasan
Trudovoye
Vladivostok
Nakhodka
Preobrazheniye
Artem

Najin

Chŏngjin

NORTH KOREA

Yeongdeok

SOUTH KOREA

Pohang

ULSAN

Korea Strait

Tsushima (Japan)

Iki

Wakkanai
Rebun-Tō
Rishiri-Tō
Teshio
Esashi
Otoineppu
Ōmu
Mombetsu
Yūbetsu
Abashiri-Wan
Abashiri
Ostrov Kunashiri
Rausu Dake
Embetsu
Kitami-Sammyaku
Engaru
Kussharo-Ko
Habōro
Nayoro
Kitami
Shari
Nakashibetsu
Rumoi
Shibetsu
Takikawa
Asahigawa
2290 Daisetsu-Zan
Ishikari-Gawa
Ishikari-Sammyaku
Nemuro
Otaru
Akabira
2077
Hokkaidō
Kamui-Misaki
Bibai
Iwamizawa
Ebetsu
Obihiro
Poroshiri-Dake
2052
SAPPORO
Sikotu-Ko
Chitose
Hidaka-Sammyaku
Shibecha
Akkeshi
Iwanai
Toya-Ko
Tomakomai
Kushiro
Suttsu
Uchiura-Wan
Muroran
Urakawa
Samani
Setana
Yakumo
Hiroo
Erimo-misaki

Okushiri-Tō
Esashi
Esan-Misaki
Hakodate
Matsumae
Tsugaru Kaikyō
Shiriya-Zaki
Shiragami-Misaki
Ohata
Mutsu
Kanagi
Mutsu-Wan
Goshogawara
Aomori
Towada-Ko
Towada
Henashi-Misaki
Hirosaki
Odate
Hachinohe
Noshiro
Kazuno
Kuji
Oga
Iwate-San
2041
Iwaizumi
Oga-Hantō
Miyako
Akita
Omagari
1914
Morioka
Hayachine-San
Kamaishi
Honjō
Hanamaki
Mizusawa
Chōkai-San
2230
Ichinoseki
Kesennuma
Sakata
Furukawa
Ishinomaki
Tsuruoka
Gas-San
1980
Hanamaki
SENDAI
Sendai-Wan
Murakami
Yamagata
Sōma
Aikawa
Ryōtsu
Nagai
Haranomachi
Sado
Niigata
Shibata
Fukushima
Kōriyama
Niitsu
Higashijima-San
2024
Sanjo
Aizuwakamatsu
Iwaki
Nagaoka
Inawashiro-Ko
Sukagawa
Kitaibaraki
Wajima
Tōkamachi
Tajima
Shirane-San Tanakura
Hitachi
Suzu-Misaki
Echigo-Sammyaku
2578
Yaita
Nanao
Suzu-Wan
Nagano
Kusatsu
Mito
Toyama-Wan
Takada
Kiryū
Utsunomiya
Hakui
Himi
Toyama
Maebashi
Oyama
Tsuchiura
Hodaka-Dake
Takasaki
Kawagoe
Takaoka
3190
Takayama
Matsumoto
Kumagaya
Honshū
Kanazawa
Haku-San
Hida-Sammyaku
Kantō-Sanchi
8412
Komatsu
2702
Ina Ōmaki
3063
Kōfu
TŌKYŌ
Funabashi
Fukui
Takefu
3192
Iida
Fuji-San
3776
KAWASAKI
Chiba
Echizen-Misaki
Gero
YOKOHAMA
Ichihara
Kyō-ga-Saki
Wakasa-Wan
Gifu
Odawara
Yokosuka
Tsuruga
Ōgaki
Ichinomiya
Fuji
Numazu
Tateyama
Tottori
Toyooka
Obama
Ichinomiya
Shizuoka
Itō
Nojima-Zaki
Matsue
Yonago
Maizuru
NAGOYA
Toyota
Hamamatsu
Ō-Shima
Izu-Shotō
Izumo
Dai-Sen
1712
Fukuchiyama
Ayabe
Otsu
Okazaki
Suruga-Wan
Niu-Jima
Ōda
Chugoku-Sanchi
Tsuyama
KYŌTO
Yokkaichi
Toyohashi
Irō-Zaki
Miyoshi
Nishinomiya
Higashiōsaka
Iwata
Miyake-Jima
9076
Hamada
Okayama
KŌBE
OSAKA Matsusaka
Masuda
Fuchū
Amagasaki
Izumi-Sano
Ise-Wan
Omae-Zaki
Aoga-Shima
HIROSHIMA
Fukuyama
Takamatsu
Wakayama
Daiō-Misaki
Hagi
Iwakuni
Kure
Marugame
Awaji-Shima
Owase
Yamaguchi
Tokuyama
Imabari
Ikeda
Naruto
Tokushima
1915
Kii-Sanchi
Hachijō-Jima
Katsumoto
Shimonoseki
Hōfu
Matsuyama
Kyushu-Sanchi
Anan
Gobō
Shingū
Nogata
Ube
Shikoku-Sanchi
Tsurugi-San
Nankoku
Mugi
Tanabe
KITAKYŪSHŪ
Bungotakada
Kōchi
Kushimoto
Shio-no-Misaki
FUKUOKA
Buzen
Beppu
Yawatahama
Tosa-Wan
Muroto
Karatsu
Kurume
Ōita
Uwajima
Shikoku
Muroto-Misaki
Imari
Saga
Saiki
Nakamura
Gotō-Rettō
Omuta
Kuju-San
1787
Sukumo
Sasebo
Isahaya
Kumamoto
Ashizuri-Zaki
Fukue-Shima
Nagasaki
Yatsushiro
Nobeoka
Amakusa-Shotō
Hondo
Hyūga
Ushibuka
Kyūshū
Koshiki-Rettō
Minamata
Miyazaki
Kurino
Sendai
Miyakonojō
Kagoshima
Nichinan
Makurazaki
Kanoya
Ibusuki
Sata-Misaki

SEA

OF

JAPAN

(EAST SEA)

JAPAN

Uleungdo (S. Korea)

Liancourt Rocks (Dokdo, Takeshima)

Oki-Shotō (Japan)

PACIFIC OCEAN

Nampō-Shotō

Projection: Conical with two standard parallels

East from Greenwich

COPYRIGHT PHILIP'S

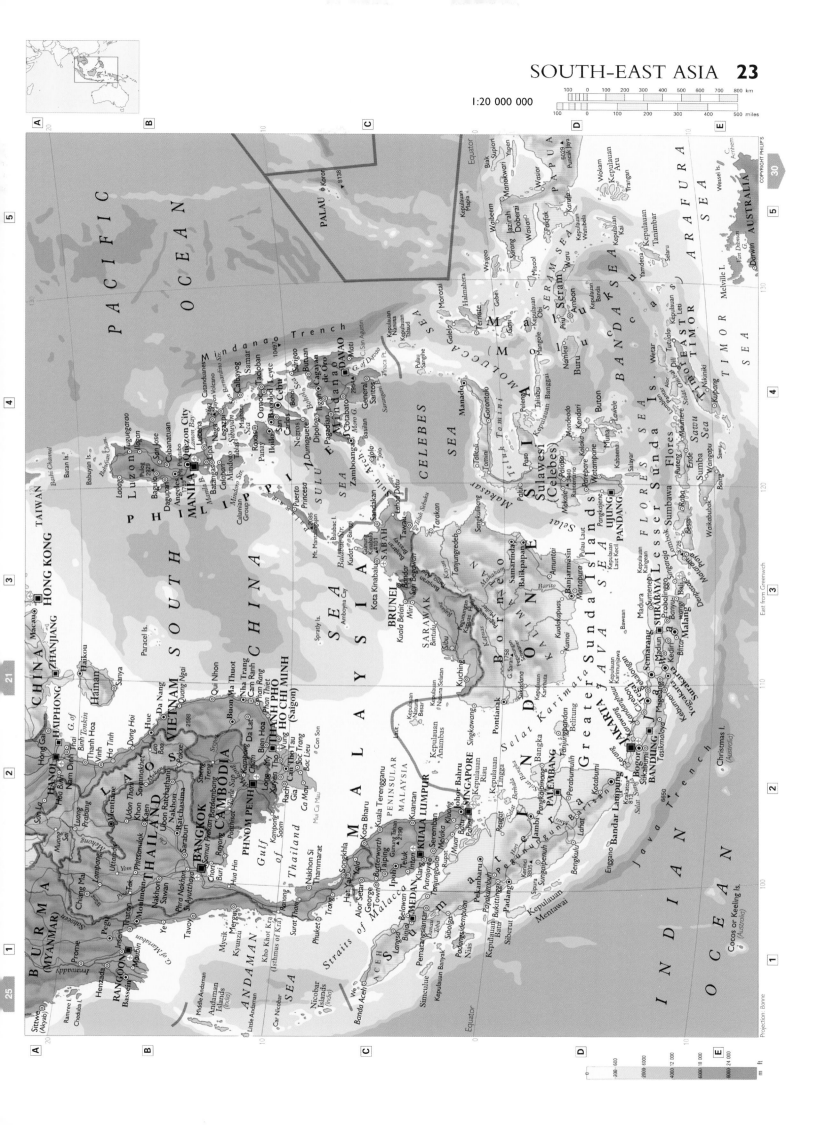

1:20 000 000

1:17 500 000

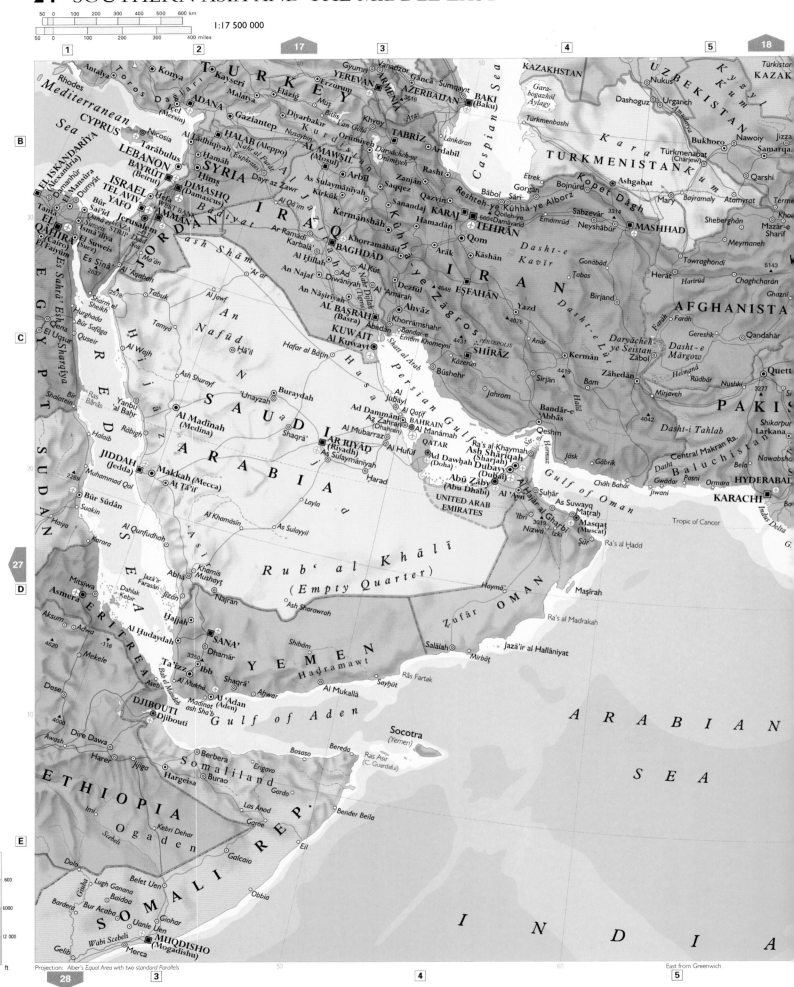

Projection: Alber's Equal Area with two standard Parallels

East from Greenwich

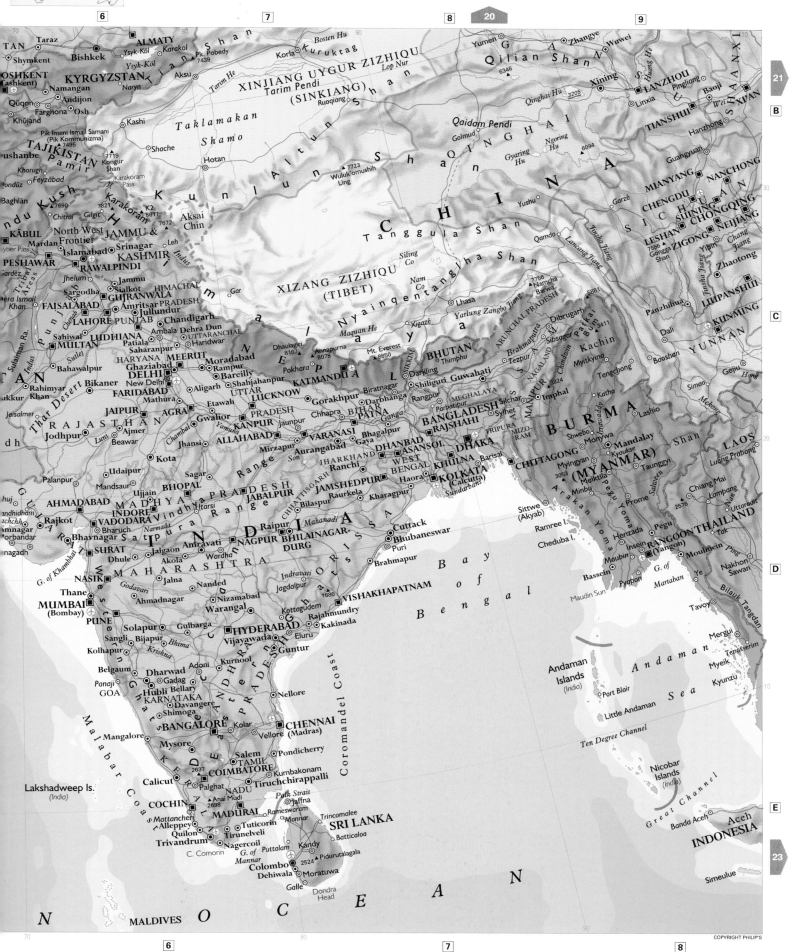

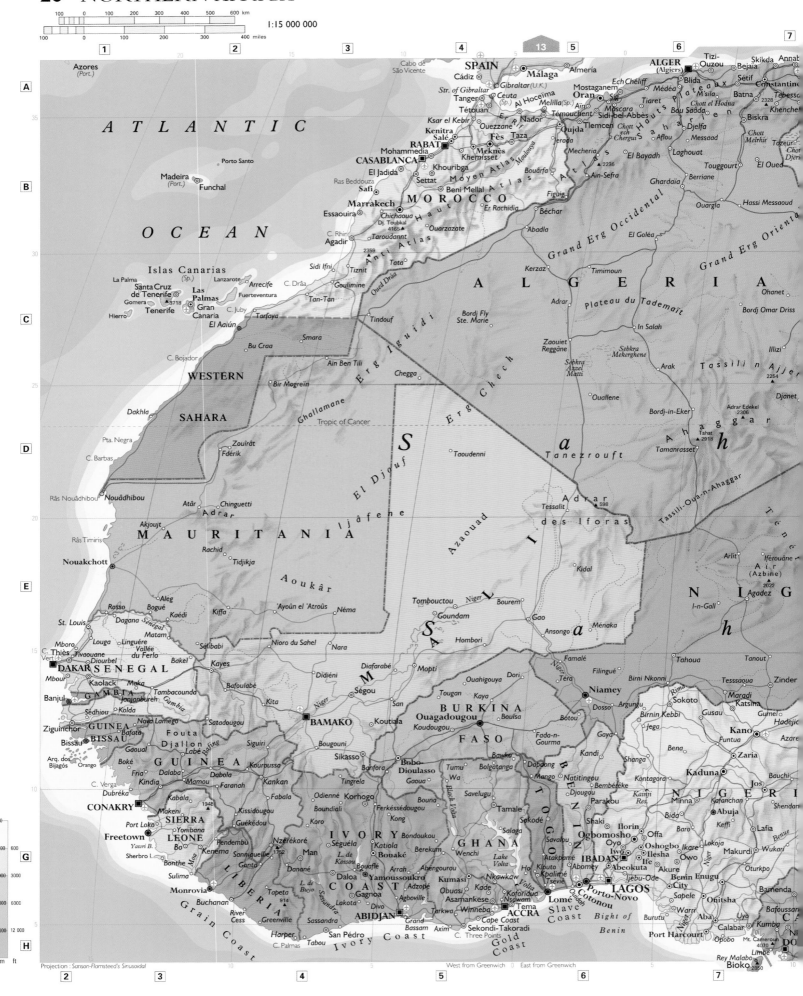

100 0 100 200 300 400 500 600 km
1:15 000 000
100 0 100 200 300 400 miles

ATLANTIC

OCEAN

Azores
(Port.)

Madeira
(Port.) Funchal

Porto Santo

SPAIN
Cabo de
São Vicente
Cádiz Málaga Almería
Str. of Gibraltar Gibraltar (U.K.)
Tanger Ceuta (Sp.) Al Hoceima Melilla (Sp.)
Tétouan Nador
Ksar el Kebir Oujda
Quezzane
Kenitra Fès Taza
Salé Meknès
RABAT
Mohammedia Khemisset
CASABLANCA
El Jadida Khouribga
Settat Beni Mellal
Safi MOROCCO
Marrakech Er Rachidia
Essaouira Chichaoua Béchar
Dj. Toubkal Ouarzazate Abadla
4165 Taroudannt
C. Rhir Anti Atlas
Agadir 2359
Sidi Ifni Tata
Tiznit Tindouf
Goulimine Oued Drâa
Tan-Tan

ALGER
(Algiers) Tizi-
Ouzou Skikda Annaba
Blida Bejaia Sétif
Constantine
Médéa M'sila Batna
Oran Mostaganem Tébessa
Sig Sidi-bel-Abbès Bou Saâda Khenchela
Moscara Tiaret Biskra
Tlemcen El Bayadh Touggourt El Oued
Mecheria Ghardaïa Berriane
Figuig Ain-Sefra Ouargla Hassi Messaoud
Grand Erg Occidental Grand Erg Oriental
El Goléa
Kerzaz Timimoun Ohanet
Adrar Plateau du Tademaït Bordj Omar Driss
Bordj Fly Ste. Marie In Salah
Zaouiet Reggâne Illizi
Arak Tassili n'Ajjer
Ouallene 2254
Bordj-in-Eker Djanet
Adrar Edekel 2306
Tamanrasset Ahaggar
Tahat 2918

ALGERIA

Islas Canarias (Sp.)
La Palma Lanzarote Arrecife
Santa Cruz de Tenerife Fuerteventura
Gomera Las Palmas
Tenerife Gran Canaria
Hierro C. Juby
El Aaiún Tarfaya
C. Bojador
Bu Craa Smara
WESTERN Ain Ben Tili Chegga
Bir Mogreïn
SAHARA Erg Iguidi Erg Chech
Dakhla
Tropic of Cancer
Pta. Negra Zouîrât
Fdérik Taoudenni
C. Barbas
El Djouf Tanezrouft
Râs Nouâdhibou Nouâdhibou Adrar des Iforas
Atâr Chinguetti Tessalit 598
MAURITANIA
Rachid Ijâfene Kidal
Akjoujt Tidjikja
Râs Timiris Aoukâr Azaouad
Nouakchott Kidal
Aleg Arlit
Rosso Bogué Néma Iférouâne
St. Louis Kaédi 'Ayoûn el 'Atroûs Aïr (Azbine)
Dagana Kiffa Agadez 2022
Louga Matam Tombouctou I-n-Gall
Mboro Linguére Niger Bourem
C. Thiès Vallée Nioro du Sahel Gao Tahoua
DAKAR Diourbel du Ferlo Nara Goundam Ansongo Ménaka Tanout
SENEGAL Sâbabi Hombori Tessaoua
Mbour Bakel Didiéni Filingué Birni Nkonni Zinder
Kaolack Méka Famalé Tahoua
GAMBIA Tambacounda Mopti Téra NIGER
Banjul Kayes Ségou Niamey Maradi Katsina
Sédhiou Kolda Ouahigouya Dori Dosso Sokoto
Ziguinchor Kita San Kaya Argungu Gusau
GUINEA Satadougou BAMAKO Koutiala Tougan BURKINA Gaya Jega Zaria
BISSAU Bafatá Koudougou OUAGADOUGOU Boulsa Birnin Kebbi Kano
Bissau Nova Lamego Siguiri Bougouni FASO Fada-n-Gourma Kontagora Azare
Arq. dos Gaoual Sikasso Bawku Kandi Minna Hadejia
Bijagós Boké Kouroussa Banfora Tumu Bolgatanga Mango Bena Kaduna
C. Verga Fouta Kankan Bobo- Bida
GUINEA Fria Dalaba Dioulasso Goua Wa Natitingou Bauchi
Dubréka Kindia Djallon Labé Tingrela Savelugu Bembéréke Jos
CONAKRY Mamou Odienné Korhogo Bouna Djougou Kainji Res. Minna Kafanchan
Kabala 1948 Faranah Bondoukou Savalou Abuja Shendan
Port Loko Fabala Katiola Tamale Parakou Baro Keffi
SIERRA Makeni Kissidougou Séguéla Tale Sokodé Lafia
Freetown Guékédou Man Bouaké BENIN Shaki Ilorin Lokoja Makurdi
LEONE Pendembu 1752 IVORY Berekum Wenchi Savalou Ogbomosho Offa Wukari
Bo Nzérékoré L. de Katiola Abomey Iwo Oshogbo Ikare Owo Oturkpo
Sherbro I. Kenema Ganta Kossou GHANA Ho Abeokuta Ilesha Ife NIGERIA
Sulima COAST Daloa Lake Klouto Ibadan Ijebu-Ode Benin Enugu
Monrovia Tapeta Yamoussoukro Volta Koforidua LAGOS City
Buchanan 914 Gagnoa Kumasi Kade Tsévié Porto-Novo Onitsha
River LIBERIA Abengourou Obuasi Nkawkaw Nsawam Cotonou Sapele
Cess Divo Asamankese Winneba Lomé Warri Aba Calabar
Greenville Sassandra Agboville ACCRA Tema Slave Coast Port Harcourt
ABIDJAN Lakota Cape Coast Bight of
Harper Sekondi-Takoradi Benin Burutu
San Pédro Grand Bassam Axim Gold Coast
C. Palmas Tabou Ivory Coast C. Three Points
Grain Coast West from Greenwich East from Greenwich
Mt. Cameroun 4070 Rey Malabo
Bioko 2260

Projection : Sanson-Flamsteed's Sinusoidal

m ft
0
200 600
1000 3000
2000 6000
4000 12 000

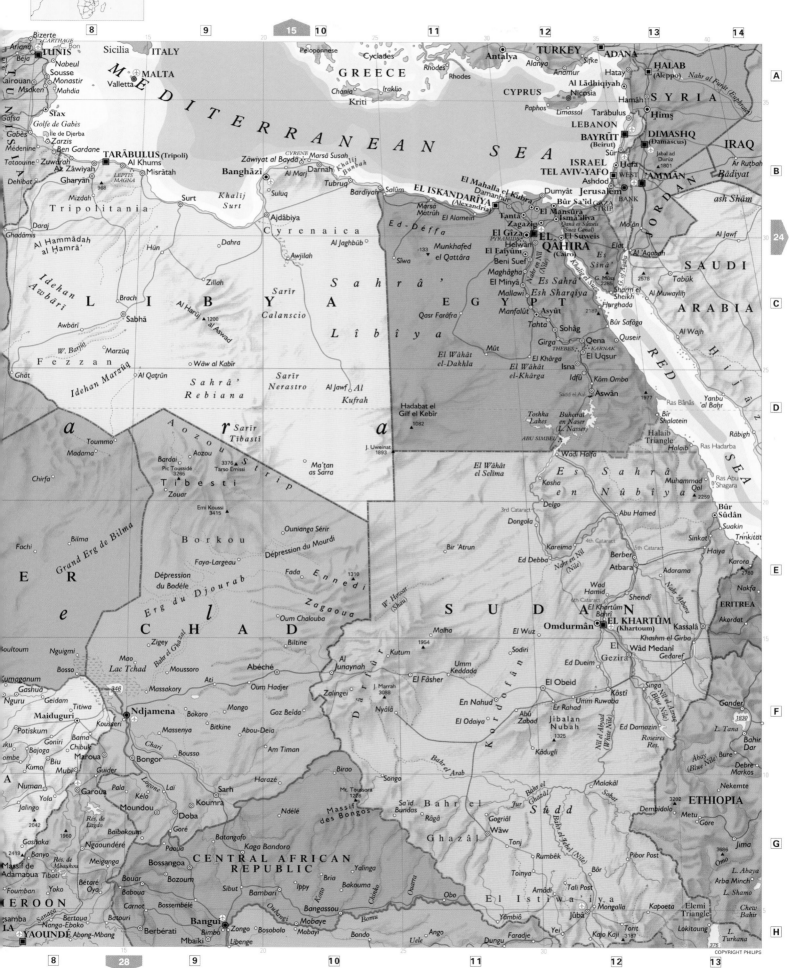

MADAGASCAR
On same scale

INDIAN OCEAN

INDIAN OCEAN

ATLANTIC OCEAN

1:20 000 000

Projection: Lambert's Equivalent Azimuthal

East from Greenwich

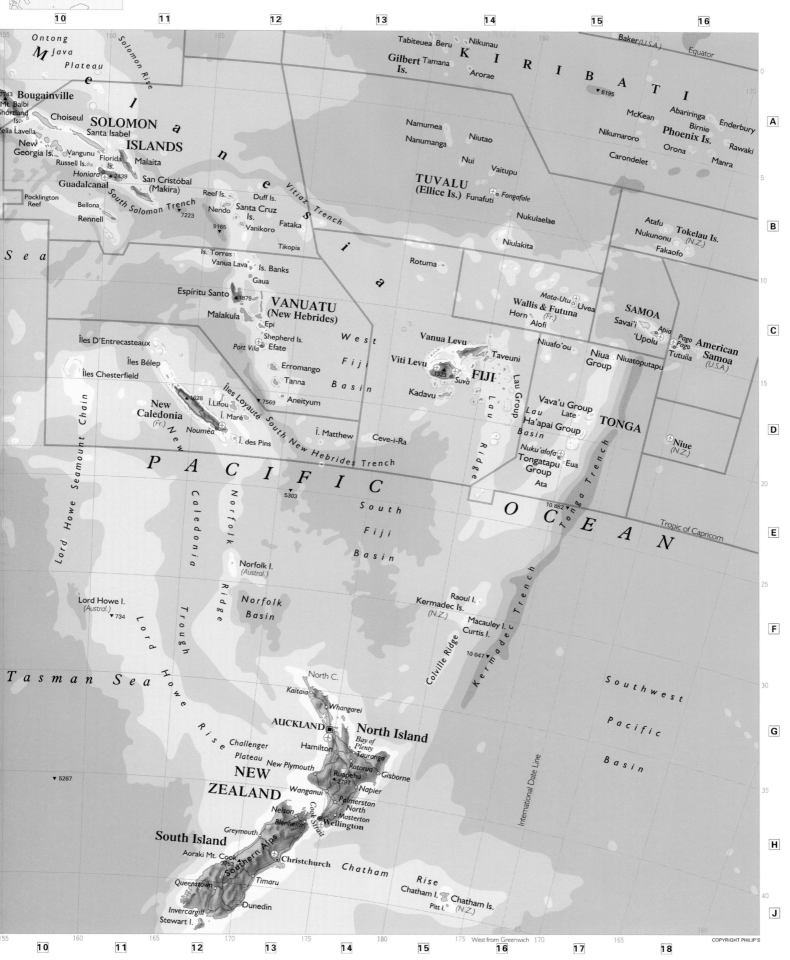

Melanesia

Ontong
Java
Plateau

Solomon Rise

2743 Bougainville
Mt. Balbi
Shortland
Is.
Choiseul
Santa Isabel
SOLOMON
Vella Lavella
New
Georgia Is.   Vangunu
Russell Is.   Florida
Honiara ▲2439   Is.   Malaita
Guadalcanal   ISLANDS
San Cristóbal
(Makira)
Pocklington
Reef
Bellona
Rennell

South Solomon Trench   7223

Sea

Vitiaz Trench

Reef Is.   Duff Is.
Nendo
9165   Santa Cruz
Vanikoro   Is.
Fataka

Tikopia

Is. Torres
Vanua Lava   Is. Banks
Gaua
Espíritu Santo   ▲1879
Malakula   VANUATU
(New Hebrides)
Epi
Shepherd Is.
Port Vila   Efate
Erromango
Tanna
Aneityum   7569

West

Fiji

Basin

Tabiteuea Beru   Nikunau
Gilbert Tamana
Is.   Arorae

KIRIBATI

▼6195

Namumea
Nanumanga   Niutao

Nui   Vaitupu

TUVALU
(Ellice Is.)   Funafuti   Fongafale

Nukulaelae

Niulakita

Rotuma

Mata-Utu   Uvea
Wallis & Futuna
Horn   (Fr.)
Alofi

Vanua Levu   Taveuni
Viti Levu   1323
Suva   FIJI
Kadavu

Ceve-i-Ra

Baker(U.S.A.)   Equator

McKean   Abariringa
Nikumaroro   Birnie   Enderbury
Phoenix Is.
Orona   Rawaki
Carondelet   Manra

Atafu   Tokelau Is.
Nukunonu   (N.Z.)
Fakaofo

SAMOA
Savai'i   Apia   Pago
'Upolu   Pago   American
Tutuila   Samoa
Niuafo'ou   (U.S.A.)
Niua   Niuatoputapu
Group   Late
Vava'u Group   TONGA
Lau   Ha'apai Group
Basin   Niue
(N.Z.)
Nuku'alofa
Tongatapu   Eua
Group
Ata

Îles D'Entrecasteaux
Îles Bélep
Îles Chesterfield

New
Caledonia
(Fr.)   1628   Î. Lifou
Nouméa   Îles Loyauté
Î. Maré
Î. des Pins
Î. Matthew

South New Hebrides Trench

PACIFIC

5303

South

Fiji

Basin

Lau Group

Lau Ridge

Tonga Trench

10 882

OCEAN

Tropic of Capricorn

Lord Howe Seamount Chain

Caledonia
Trough

Norfolk
Ridge

Norfolk I.
(Austral.)

Lord Howe I.
(Austral.)   734

Lord Howe Rise

Norfolk
Basin

Raoul I.
Kermadec Is.
(N.Z.)
Macauley I.
Curtis I.

10 047

Colville Ridge

Kermadec Trench

Southwest

Pacific

Basin

Tasman Sea

5267

North C.
Kaitaia
Whangarei
AUCKLAND   North Island
Hamilton   Bay of
Challenger   Plenty
Plateau   New Plymouth   Tauranga
Rotorua
Ruapehu   Gisborne
NEW   2797
Wanganui   Napier
ZEALAND   Palmerston
North
Nelson   Masterton
Greymouth   Blenheim   Wellington
South Island   Cook Strait
Aoraki Mt. Cook   Christchurch   Chatham
3763   Southern Alps
Queenstown   Timaru   Rise
Chatham I.   Chatham Is.
Invercargill   Pitt I.   (N.Z.)
Dunedin
Stewart I.

International Date Line

West from Greenwich

1:8 000 000

National Parks

1:6 000 000

50 0 50 100 150 200 km
50 0 50 100 150 miles

NORTH ISLAND

C. Reinga
North C.
C. Maria van Diemen
Houhora Heads
Rangaunu B.
Doubtless B.
Whangaroa Harb.
Ahipara B.
Kaitaia
Tauroa Pt.
Rawene
I. Okaihau
Waitangi
B. of Islands
C. Brett
Opua
Hokianga Harbour
Waipoua Forest
Dargaville
Kaikohe
Hikurangi
Kaikohe
Whangarei
Whangarei Harb.
Bream Hd.
Bream B.
Waipu
Little Barrier I.
Warkworth
C. Rodney
Great Barrier I.
Kaipara Harbour
Helensville
C. Colville
Cuvier I.
Hauraki Gulf
Coromandel
Whitianga
Takapuna
AUCKLAND
Manukau
Papakura
Thames
Whangamata
Pukekohe
Whangamata
Mayor I.
Waiuku
Mercer
Paeroa
Waihi
Waikato
Huntly
Te Aroha
Mount Maunganui
Te Puke
Raglan
Morrinsville
Tauranga
Bay of Plenty
Hamilton
Cambridge
Whakatane
Whakaari (White I.)
Runaway
Te Awamutu
Kawhia
Kawerau
Taneatua
East C.
Kawhia Harbour
Otorohanga
Putaruru
Rotorua
Rotorua
L. Tarawera
Opotiki
Hikurangi 1753
Te Kuiti
Tokoroa
Murupara
Raukumara Ra.
Waipiro
Mokau
Kinleith
Mokai
L. Taupo
Waikaremoana
Motu
Tolaga Bay
North Taranaki Bight
Wairakei
UREWERA
Waitara
Ongarue
Taupo
Taumarunui
Turangi
Tarawera
Nuhaka
Gisborne
Poverty Bay
New Plymouth
Whangamomona
WHANGANUI
Waikokopu
Inglewood
EGMONT
Ruapehu 2797
Waikaremoana
Mahia Pen.
Mt. Taranaki or Mt. Egmont 2518
Stratford
Ohakune
TONGARIRO
Wairoa
C. Egmont
Eltham
Raetihi
Waiouru
Bay View
Opunake
Kaponga
Hawera
Taihape
Ruahine Ra.
Napier
South Taranaki Bight
Waverley
Mangaweka
C. Kidnappers
Patea
Hastings
Wanganui
Hunterville
Waipawa
Marton
Halcombe
Waipukurau
Bulls
Feilding
Dannevirke
Palmerston North
Woodville
Foxton
Shannon
Pahiatua
Levin
C. Turnagain
Paraparaumu
 Eketahuna
Otaki
Pelorus
Kapiti I.
Masterton
Upper Hutt
Featherston
Carterton
Petone
Greytown
Lower Hutt
Martinborough
Wellington
Wairarapa
Cook Strait

SOUTH ISLAND

C. Farewell
Golden B.
Collingwood
D'Urville I.
Takaka
ABEL TASMAN
KAHURANGI
Tasman B.
Karamea
Tasman Mts.
Motueka
Karamea Bight
Matiri Ra.
Nelson
Havelock
Seddonville
Tadmor
Richmond
Picton
Granity
Murchison
Wakefield
Lyell
Inangahua
Waimea
Westport
Rotoroa
NELSON LAKES
Blenheim
PAPAROA
Mt. Travers 2885
Tapuae-o-Uenuku
Seddon
Punakaiki
Reefton
Spenser Mts.
Ward
Blackball
Lewis Pass
Hanmer Springs
Clarence
Runanga
Waiau
Kaikoura
Greymouth
Stillwater
L. Brunner
Kaikoura
Kumara
Jacksons
Culverden
Hokitika
ARTHUR'S PASS
Waikari
Waiau
Ross
Arthur's P.
Hurunui
Waipara
Amberley
Pegasus Bay
Abut Hd.
Rangiora
Oxford
Kaiapoi
South Island
WESTLAND
Springfield
New Brighton
Aoraki
Mt Cook 3753
MT COOK
Whitecliffs
Christchurch
Lincoln
Lyttelton
Jackson B.
Okuru
Haast
L. Tekapo
Methven
Staveley
Banks Pen.
Little River
Akaroa
MOUNT ASPIRING
Mt. Aspiring 3027
Twizel
Canterbury Plains
Ashburton
Rakaia
L. Ohau
Fairlie
L. Pukaki
Rakaia
Southbridge
Milford Sd.
Earnslaw 2818
Wanaka
L. Hawea
Timaru
Sutherland Falls
St. Andrews
Bligh Sound
Milford Sound
Wanaka
Kurow
Waimate
George Sound
Queenstown
Arrowtown
Cromwell
Tokarahi
Canterbury Bight
Wakatipu
Clyde
Kakanui Mts.
Oamaru
Secretary I.
Alexandra
Maheno
Doubtful Sd.
Te Anau
Kingston
Garvie Mts.
Roxburgh
Hampden
Dunback
Palmerston
FIORDLAND
L. Te Anau
Umbrella Mts.
Otago
Waikouaiti
Manapouri
Mossburn
Lumsden
Clutha
L. Mahinerangi
Port Chalmers
Breaksea Sd.
L. Manapouri
Eyre Mts.
Otago Harbour
Resolution I.
Ohai
Edievale
C. Saunders
Dusky Sd.
Nightcaps
Tapanui
Lawrence
Dunedin
Southland
Kelso
Milton
Clifden
Winton
Clinton
Preservation Inlet
Tuatapere
Hedgehope
Ohai
Balclutha
Te Waewae B.
Orepuki
Gore
Mataura
Kaitangata
Chalky Inlet
Riverton
Nugget Pt.
Invercargill
Tokanui
Owaka
Bluff
South Invercargill
Ruapuke I.
Wyndham
Tahakopa
Solander I.
Foveaux Str.
Halfmoon Bay
Stewart I. (Rakiura)
RAKIURA
Port Pegasus
South West C.

TASMAN SEA

PACIFIC OCEAN

Projection : Conical with two standard parallels
East from Greenwich

National Parks

SAMOA
AMERICAN SAMOA
Savai'i
Apia
Upolu
Pago Pago
Tutuila
West from Greenwich

Wallis & Futuna (Fr.)
Futuna
Niuafo'ou (Tonga)
Thikombia
Labasa
Vanua Levu
FIJI
Taveuni
Yasawa Group
Vanua Balavu
Koro
Lautoka 1323
Levuka
Nandi
Ovalau
Lau Group
Viti Levu
Gau
Suva
Koro Sea
Lakeba
Moala
Kadavu
Vatoa
Vava'u
PACIFIC OCEAN
Tofua
TONGA (Friendly Is.)
Tongatapu
Nuku'alofa

FIJI AND TONGA
1:12 000 000

50 0 50 100 150 200 km
50 0 50 100 150 miles

East from Greenwich
West from Greenwich

Equatorial Scale 1:54 000 000

B RUSSIA

Yekaterinburg
Novosibirsk
Irkutsk
Oz. Baykal
Chita
Okhotsk
Sea of Okhotsk
Poluostrov Kamchatka
Komandorskiye Ostrova *(Russia)*
Shirshov Ridge
Near Is. (U.S.A.)
Andreanof I. *(U.S.A.)*
Berin Sea
Aleutian Basin

Moskva
Volga
Astana (Aqmola)
Semey
Ulaanbaatar
Blagoveshchensk
Amur
Khabarovsk
Sakhalin
Petropavlovsk-Kamchatskiy
7822
Aleutia
Aleutian Trench

C KAZAKHSTAN
Aral Sea
Balqash Köl
Ürümqi
MONGOLIA
Changchun
Harbin
Sapporo
Hokkaidō
Hakodate
La Pérouse Str.
Kurilskiye Ostrova (Russia)
Kuril-Kamchatka Trench
10,542
Northwest
Chinook Trough

Toshkent
Almaty
SHENYANG
Beijing
Tianjin
Vladivostok
Sea of Japan
Honshū
Emperor Trough
Emperor Seamount Chain

D TAJIKISTAN
CHINA
Kunlun Shan
XIZANG
Lanzhou
Taiyuan
Huang He
NORTH KOREA
Dalian
Seoul
SOUTH KOREA
Sendai
Tōkyō
Yokohama
Shatsky Rise
Pacific

AFGHANISTAN
Kābul
Srinagar
PAKISTAN
Xi'an
Chengdu
Chongqing
Nanjing
Wuhan
Shanghai
Yellow Sea
Qingdao
Kyōto
Ōsaka
JAPAN
Nagoya
Fuji-San 3776
Shikoku
Kyūshū
10,554
Japan Trench

E Lahore
Delhi
Kanpur
Ganga
NEPAL
Mt. Everest 8850
Lhasa
Brahmaputra
Chang J.
Changsha
Hangzhou
East China Sea
Kunming
Fuzhou
Taipei
Okinawa
Ryūkyū-rettō (Japan)
Guangzhou
Hong Kong
Macau
Kyushu-Palau Ridge
Shikoku-Ozima-Ridge
Iwo-Jima *(Japan)*
Ogasawara Gunto *(Japan)*
Kazan-Rettō *(Japan)*
Minami-Tori-Shima *(Japan)*
Midway Is. *(U.S.A.)*
Lisianski I. *(U.S.A.)*

Kolkata (Calcutta)
Dhaka
Mandalay
Irrawaddy
TAIWAN
Philippine Sea
Basin
Mid-Pacific Seamou
Wake I. *(U.S.A.)*

F INDIA
Hyderabad
Bay of Bengal
BURMA
Rangoon
Salween
LAOS
Hanoi
Hainan
C. Engano
Luzon
Paracel Is.
Manila
Philippine Basin
West Mariana Basin
NORTHERN MARIANAS *(U.S.A.)*
East Mariana Basin
Tinian
Saipan
MARSHALL IS.
Eniwetak Atoll
Bikini Atoll
Ralik Chain
Ratak Chain
P
A

Chennai (Madras)
Andaman Is. *(India)*
THAILAND
Bangkok
CAMBODIA
VIETNAM
Mekong
Mindoro
PHILIPPINES
Samar
10,497
Challenger 11,022 Deep
GUAM *(U.S.A.)*
Majuro
Mariana Trench
Micronesia

G SRI LANKA
Colombo
Nicobar Is. *(India)*
G. of Thailand
Phnom Penh
Thanh Pho Ho Chi Minh
South China Sea
Palawan
Sulu Sea
Mindanao
Davao
Philippine Trench
Yap
Koror
Caroline Is.
Truk
PALAU
FED. STATES OF MICRONESIA
Pohnpei
Palikir
Jaluit I.
Central
Pacific
4191
Eaurapik Rise
Butaritari
Tarawa

H MALAYSIA
Kuala Lumpur
PEN. MALAYSIA
BRUNEI
SABAH
Celebes Sea
Maluku
Halmahera
Seram
Banda Sea
7440
PAPUA NEW GUINEA
Admiralty
New Ireland
East Caroline Basin
West Caroline Basin
Melanesian Basin
Solomon Rise
Melan
Kiri
Banaba
NAURU
Yaren
Gilbert Is.
Howland I. *(U.S.A.)*
Baker I. *(U.S.A.)*
Phoenix Is.
Abariringa
Enderbury

Singapore
Sumatera
INDONESIA
Borneo
SARAWAK
Sulawesi
Buru
Ujung Pandang
PUNCAK Jaya 5029
PAPUA
New Guinea
Bismarck Arch.
Lae
Rabaul 8940
Bougainville
New Britain
SOLOMON IS.
Honiara
Guadalcanal
Fongafale
TUVALU

J INDIAN OCEAN
Palembang
Java Sea
Jakarta
Jawa
Surabaya
Flores Sea
Bali
Flores
Sunda Trench (Java Trench)
Sumbawa
Sumba
EAST TIMOR
Arafura Sea
C. Arnhem
Darwin
Gulf of Carpentaria
Port Moresby
Torres Strait
C. York
Louisiade Arch.
Santa Cruz Is. 9165
Espíritu Santo
Port Vila
West Fiji Basin
Vanua Levu
Viti Levu
Suva
FIJI
SAMOA
Apia
Rotuma
Is. Wallis & Futuna *(Fr.)*

Ninetyeast Ridge
Wharton Basin
Christmas I. *(Austral.)*
Cocos Is. *(Austral.)*
North Australian Basin
Coral Sea Basin
Cairns
Townsville
Coral Sea
VANUATU
Îs. Chesterfield
7570
NEW CALEDONIA *(Fr.)*
Nouméa
Is. Loyauté
Nuku'alofa
TONGA
10,822
Kermadec Trench

K OCEAN
Broken Ridge
Exmouth Plateau
Broome
North West C.
AUSTRALIA
Mount Isa
Alice Springs
Rockhampton
Brisbane
Great Dividing Ra.
Middleton Basin
Lord Howe I. *(Austral.)*
Lord Howe Rise
Norfolk Ridge
New Caledonia Ridge
South Fiji Basin
Kermadec Is. *(N.Z.)*
10,047

L *Naturaliste Plateau*
Geraldton
Perth Basin
Perth
Albany
Great Australian Bight
L. Eyre
Murray
Canberra
Sydney
Mt. Kosciuszko 2230
Adelaide
South Australian Basin
Norfolk I. *(Austral.)*
Norfolk Basin
Tasman Sea
NEW ZEALAND
Auckland
Wellington

M Nouvelle Amsterdam *(Fr.)*
Îs. St. Paul *(Fr.)*
Melbourne
Bass Str.
Tasmania
Hobart
East Tasman Plateau
Tasman Basin
Aoraki Mt. Cook 3753 *(N.Z.)*
Christchurch
Dunedin
Invercargill
Chatham Rise
Chatham I. *(N.Z.)*
Bounty Trough
Bounty Is. *(N.Z.)*

N Îs. Crozet *(Fr.)*
Kerguelen *(Fr.)*
Heard I. *(Austral.)*
Kerguelen Plateau
South Tasman Rise
SOUTHERN OCEAN
Macquarie Is. *(Austral.)*
Auckland Is. *(N.Z.)*
Antipodes Is. *(N.Z.)*
Campbell I. *(N.Z.)*
Campbell Plateau

Projection: Mollweide's Homolographic

East from Greenwich

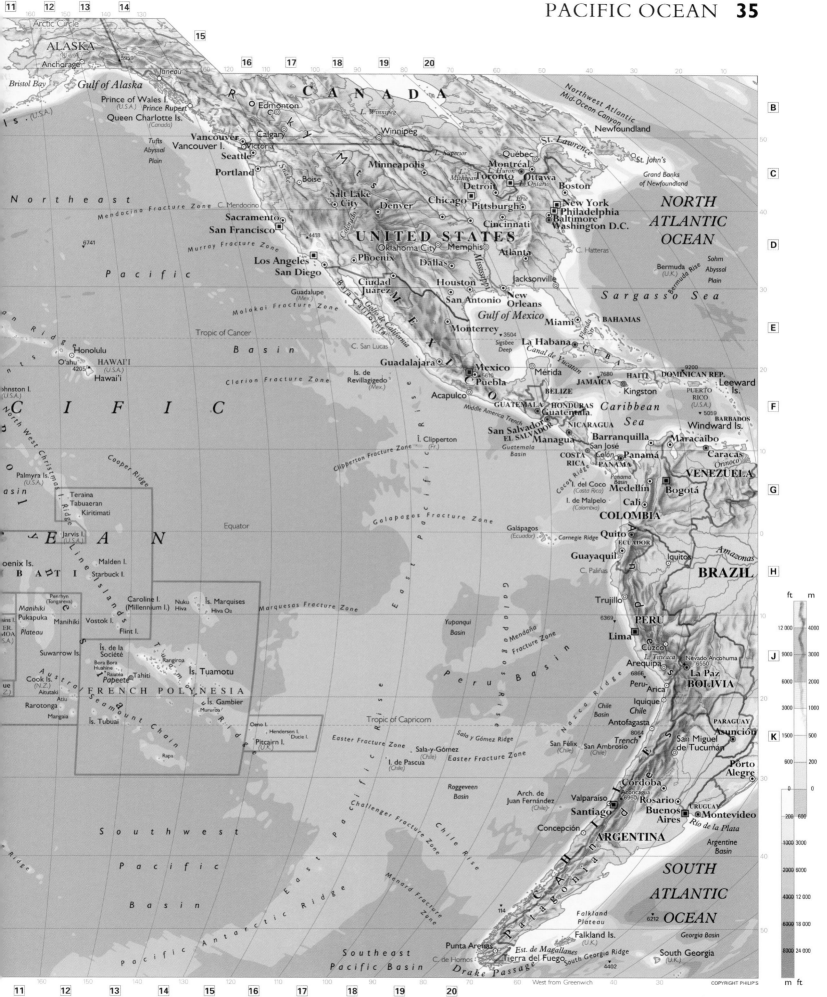

Arctic Circle

ALASKA
(U.S.A.)
Anchorage
Bristol Bay
Gulf of Alaska
Juneau
5959
Prince of Wales I.
(U.S.A.)
Prince Rupert
Queen Charlotte Is.
(Canada)

R O C K Y

C A N A D A

Edmonton

L. Winnipeg

Northwest Atlantic
Mid-Ocean Canyon

Newfoundland

B

Calgary
Winnipeg
Vancouver
Vancouver I.
Victoria
Seattle
Portland
Boise

L. Superior
St. Lawrence
Québec
Montréal
L. Huron
Toronto
Ottawa
Boston
L. Ontario
Detroit
L. Erie

St. John's

Grand Banks
of Newfoundland

C

*Tufts
Abyssal
Plain*

Snake

Salt Lake
City

Denver

Chicago
Pittsburgh

New York
Philadelphia
Baltimore
Washington D.C.

*NORTH
ATLANTIC
OCEAN*

D

N o r t h e a s t

Mendocino Fracture Zone

C. Mendocino

Sacramento
San Francisco

Colorado

Cincinnati

UNITED STATES

Memphis

Atlanta

C. Hatteras

Bermuda
(U.K.)

Bermuda Rise

Sohm
Abyssal
Plain

6741

4418

Murray Fracture Zone

Los Angeles
San Diego

Phoenix

Oklahoma City
Dallas

Houston

Jacksonville

New
Orleans

Sargasso Sea

Guadalupe
(Mex.)

Ciudad
Juárez

P a c i f i c

3504

Miami
Gulf of Mexico

BAHAMAS

E

Tropic of Cancer

Molokai Fracture Zone

Golfo de California

San Antonio

Monterrey

Sigsbee
Deep

La Habana

Canal de Yucatán

CUBA

9200

20

C. San Lucas

B a s i n

M E X I C O

Guadalajara

5610
Mexico
Puebla

Mérida

Clarion Fracture Zone

Honolulu
O'ahu
HAWAI'I
(U.S.A.)
Hawai'i

4205

Is. de
Revillagigedo
(Mex.)

5059

Acapulco

BELIZE

7680

JAMAICA

HAITI

DOMINICAN REP.

PUERTO
RICO
(U.S.A.)

Leeward
Is.

F

C I F I C

Johnston I.
(U.S.A.)

North West Christmas

Palmyra Is.
(U.S.A.)

Cooper Ridge

Î. Clipperton
(Fr.)

Middle America Trench

GUATEMALA
Guatemala

HONDURAS

San Salvador
EL SALVADOR

Managua
NICARAGUA

*Caribbean
Sea*

Kingston

5059

BARBADOS

Windward Is.

Barranquilla

Maracaibo

Caracas

Orinoco

Ridge

Line Islands

Teraina
Tabuaeran
Kiritimati

Guatemala
Basin

**COSTA
RICA**

San José

Colón
PANAMA

Panamá

Panama
Basin

I. del Coco
(Costa Rica)

Coco Ridge

VENEZUELA

G

E A N

Jarvis I.
(U.S.A.)

Phoenix Is.

Malden I.

Starbuck I.

Equator

Galápagos Fracture Zone

I. de Malpelo
(Colombia)

Medellín

Bogotá

COLOMBIA

Cali

0

K I R I B A T I

Caroline I.
(Millennium I.)

Nuku
Hiva

Îs. Marquises
Hiva O₂

Galápagos
(Ecuador)

Carnegie Ridge

Quito
ECUADOR

Guayaquil

Iquitos

Amazonas

BRAZIL

H

ains I.

ER.
SAMOA
(U.S.A.)

Manihiki
Pukapuka

Manihiki
Plateau

Penrhyn
(Tongareva)

Vostok I.

Flint I.

Marquesas Fracture Zone

*Yupanqui
Basin*

C. Palinas

Trujillo

6369

PERU

10

Suwarrow Is.

Îs. de la
Société

Bora Bora
Huahine

Îs. Tuamotu

Galápagos
Mendaña

Fracture Zone

Lima

Cuzco

East Pacific Rise

Îs. Marquises

ue
.Z.)

A Cook Is.
(N.Z.)

Raiatéa
Papeete

Tahiti

Rangiroa

FRENCH POLYNESIA

Îs. Gambier

Mururoa

P e r u B a s i n

L. Titicaca
Nevado Ancohuma
6550

Arequipa

6866
Peru-
Arica

La Paz
BOLIVIA

J

Aitutaki

Rarotonga

Mangaia

Îs. Tubuai

Seamount Chain

Ridge

Oeno I.

Tropic of Capricorn

Easter Fracture Zone

Sala y Gómez Ridge

Iquique
Chile

Antofagasta

Chile
Basin

8064
Trench

PARAGUAY

Asunción

K

Rapa

Henderson I.
Pitcairn I.
(U.K.)

Ducie I.

Sala-y-Gómez
I. de Pascua
(Chile)

Easter Fracture Zone

San Félix
(Chile)

San Ambrosio
(Chile)

San Miguel
de Tucumán

Córdoba
Aconcagua
6960

Porto
Alegre

*Roggeveen
Basin*

Arch. de
Juan Fernández
(Chile)

Chile Rise

Valparaíso
Santiago

Rosario
URUGUAY

Buenos
Aires

Montevideo

Río de la Plata

Challenger Fracture Zone

Concepción

ARGENTINA

*Argentine
Basin*

S o u t h w e s t

P a c i f i c

B a s i n

Ridge

Pacific Antarctic Ridge

East

Pacific

Ridge

Menard Fracture
Zone

114

*SOUTH
ATLANTIC
OCEAN*

6212

Falkland
Plateau

Falkland Is.
(U.K.)

Georgia Basin

South Georgia
(U.K.)

Punta Arenas

*Southeast
Pacific Basin*

Est. de Magallanes
Tierra del Fuego

C. de Hornos

South Georgia Ridge

4402

Drake Passage

ft   m

12 000   4000

9000   3000

6000   2000

3000   1000

1500   500

600   200

0   0

200   600

1000   3000

2000   6000

4000   12 000

6000   18 000

8000   24 000

m   ft

1:15 000 000

100   0   100   200   300   400   500   600 km
100   0   100   200   300   400 miles

Projection : Bonne

ALASKA
1:30 000 000

100   0   100 200 300 400 500 600 km
100   0   100   200   300   400 miles

West from Greenwich

NORTHERN CANADA
Continuation northwards on same
scale as main map

COPYRIGHT PHILIP'S

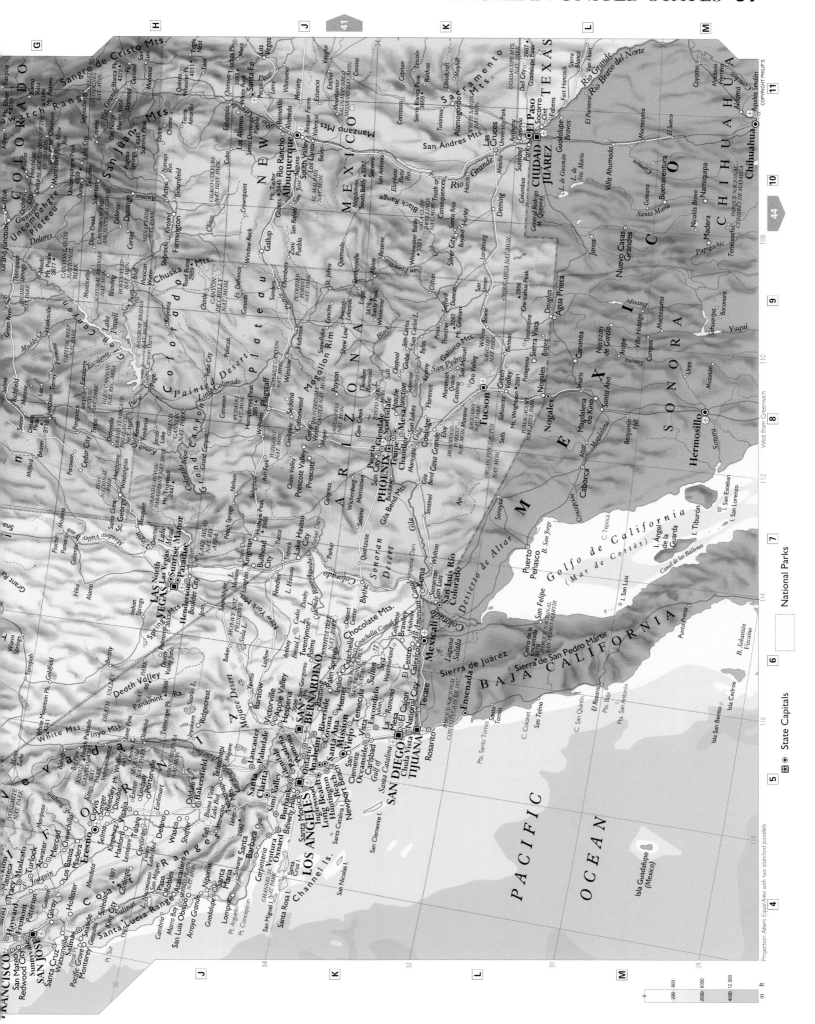

Projection: Albers Equal Area with two standard parallels

State Capitals ⊞ ⊛ National Parks

West from Greenwich

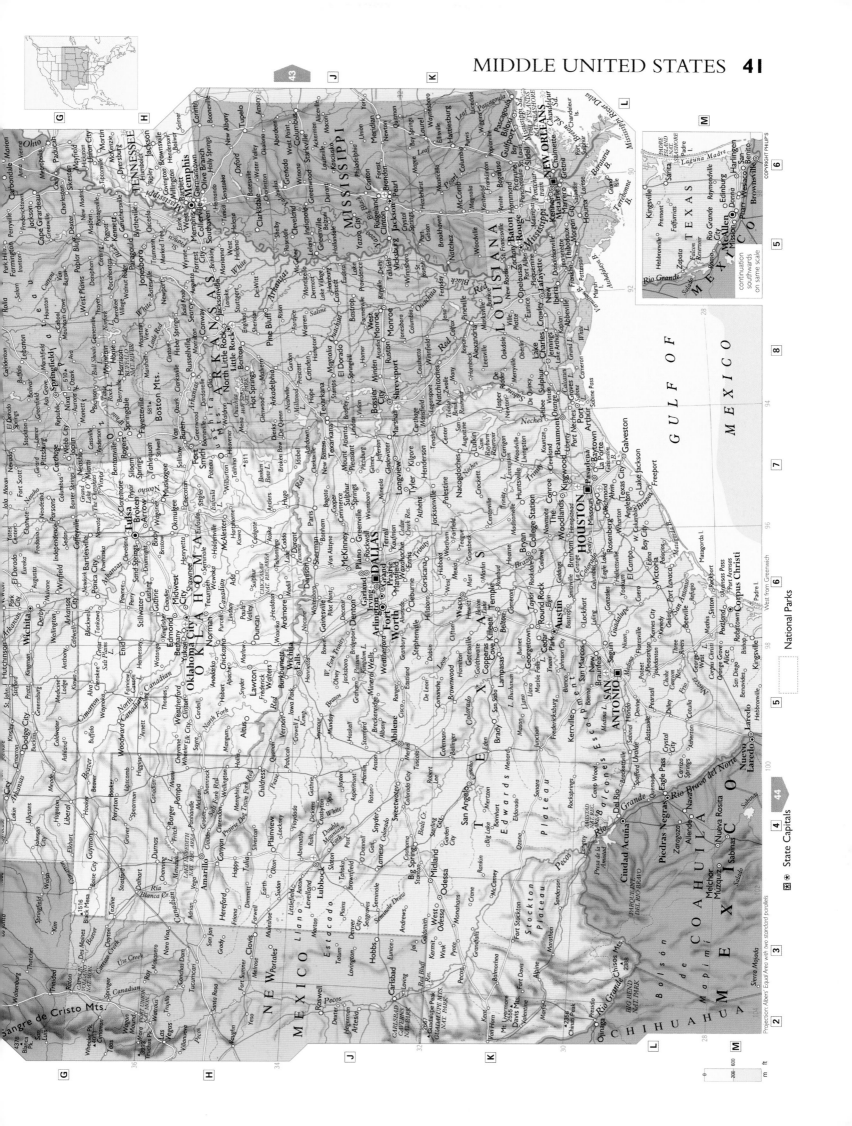

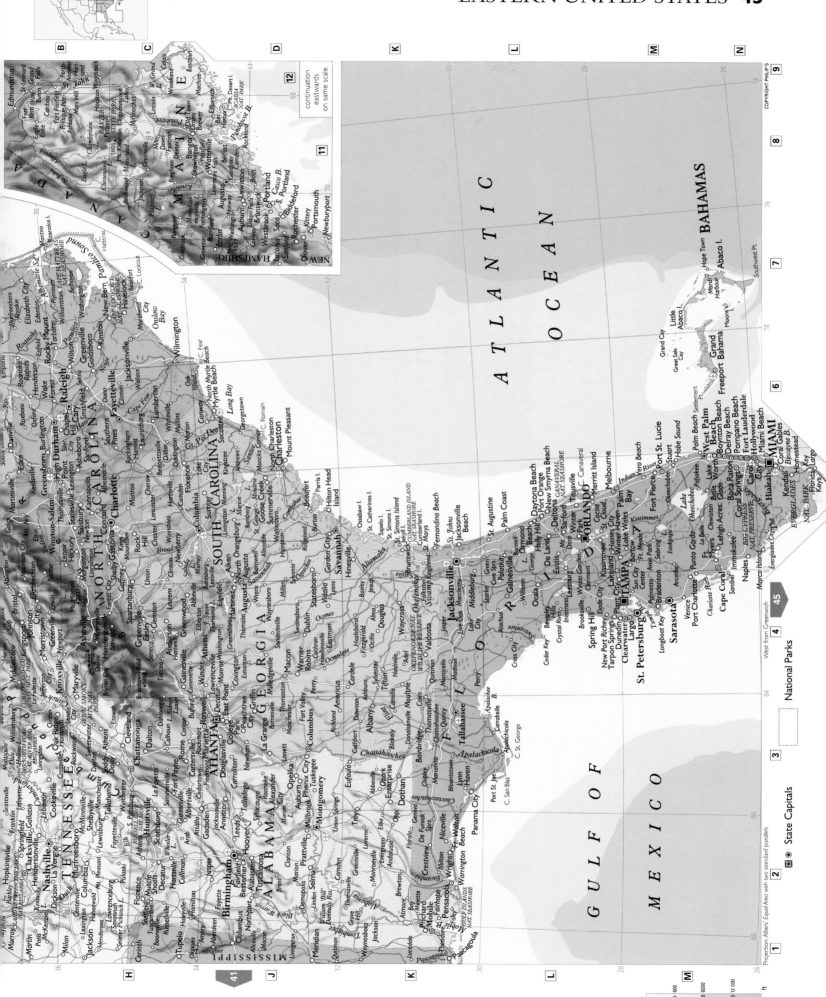

A T L A N T I C   O C E A N

G U L F   O F

M E X I C O

BAHAMAS

National Parks

State Capitals

continuation
eastwards
on the same scale

Projection: Albers Equal Area with two standard parallels

COPYRIGHT PHILIP'S

1:15 000 000

100 0 100 200 300 400 500 600 km
100 0 100 200 300 400 miles

1 **2** **3** **4** 39 **5** **6** **7**

SAN DIEGO
TIJUANA
Mexicali
Ensenada
PHOENIX
Yuma
Tucson
Casa Grande
Deming
Sonoyta
Nogales
Douglas
Agua Prieta
CIUDAD JUÁREZ
El Paso
Las Cruces
Carlsbad
Roswell
3659
Lubbock
Wichita Falls
Little Rock
Huntsville
Sherman
Greenville
Birmingham
Tuscaloosa

UNITED STATE

Abilene
Fort Worth DALLAS
Tyler
Texarkana
Shreveport
Monroe
Jackson
Meridian
Montgomery

San Felipe
3078
I. Ángel de la Guarda
I. Tiburón
Caborca
Magdalena de Kino
Hermosillo
Cananea
Nacozari
Nuevo Casas Grandes
Madera
Ojinaga
Del Rio
Pecos
Fort Stockton
San Angelo
Waco
Bryan
Austin
HOUSTON
Beaumont
Lake Charles
Lafayette
Baton Rouge
Mobile
Pensacola
NEW ORLEANS
S. San Blas

Bahía Sebastián Vizcaíno
Pta. Baja
Pta. Falsa
Rosarito
Santa Rosalía
Ciudad Obregón
Navojoa
Huatabampo
Chihuahua
Cuauhtémoc
Delicias
Ciudad Camargo
Jiménez
3050
Hidalgo del Parral
Villa Ahumada
Nueva Rosita
Sabinas
Monclova
San Pedro de las Colonias
Piedras Negras
Eagle Pass
Ciudad Acuña
2896
San Antonio
Victoria
Galveston
Matagorda I.
Corpus Christi
Padre I.

Baja California

C. San Lázaro
B. de La Paz
La Paz
2164
C. San Lucas
Cabo San Lucas
Culiacán
Los Mochis
Guasave
Guamúchil
El Fuerte
Topolobampo
Gómez Palacio
Durango
TORREÓN
Saltillo
MONTERREY
Reynosa
McAllen
Matamoros
Brownsville
Laguna Madre
Nuevo Laredo
Laredo
Falcon Res.

GULF OF MEXIC

Mazatlán
Rosario
El Salto
Sombrerete
Concepción del Oro
Matehuala
3540
Montemorelos
Linares
San Fernando
Ciudad Victoria
Tropic of Cancer
3664

Islas Marías
Escuinapa
Acaponeta
Tuxpan
Tepic
Jerez
Fresnillo
Zacatecas
Charcas
2980
San Luis Potosí
Ciudad Mante
Ciudad Madero
Tampico
Ciudad Valles
Yucatan

Is. de Revillagigedo (Mex.)
Puerto Vallarta
C. Corrientes
GUADALAJARA
Ameca
Aguascalientes
LEÓN
Guanajuato
Irapuato
Querétaro
Celaya
Pachuca
Tulancingo
Poza Rica
Papantla
Tuxpan
Pánuco
C. Rojo
Magozal
Progreso
Mérida
Motul
Tizimín
C. Catoche
Cancún
Cozumel
I. de Cozumel
Valladolid
Peto
Ticul

Golfo de Campeche
Campeche
Champotón
Laguna de Términos
Ciudad del Carmen
Escárcega
Chetumal
Corozal
Felipe Carrillo Puerto
Yucatán

Ciudad Guzmán
Nevado de Colima 4240
Colima
Zamora
L. de Chapala
Morelia
MÉXICO
TOLUCA
Popocatépetl 5452
Cuernavaca
5610 Pico de Orizaba
Xalapa
Veracruz
Córdoba
Orizaba
San Andrés Tuxtla
Coatzacoalcos
Villahermosa
Palenque
Belize City
Ambergris Cay
Turneffe Is.
BELIZE
Belmopan
Dangriga

Manzanillo
Tecomán
Uruapan
Lázaro Cárdenas
Balsas
Iguala
PUEBLA
3550
Tlapa
Minatitlán
Istmo de Tehuantepec
Tuxtla Gutiérrez
San Cristóbal de las Casas
Comitán
Puerto Cortés
Puerto Barrios
Gulf of Honduras
Roatán
Tela
La Ceiba
Trujillo

Chilpancingo
Chilapa
3550
Acapulco
5448
Ometepec
Tlaxiaco
3397
Oaxaca
Tehuantepec
Juchitán
3139
Salina Cruz
Tonalá
Huixtla
4093
GUATEMALA
Cobán
8834
San Pedro Sula
HONDURAS
Comayagua
Juticalpa
Tegucigalpa

G. de Tehuantepec
Tapachula
Quezaltenango
Escuintla
GUATEMALA
Santa Ana
Sonsonate
San Vicente
SAN SALVADOR
San Miguel
Ocotal
Matagal
NICAR
MANAGUA

PACIFIC

EL SALVADOR
6662
La Unión
G. de Fonseca
Chinandega
León
Masaya
Granada
Lago de Nicaragua
Rivas

OCEAN

Pen. de Nicoya
Puntaren

I. del Coco (Costa Rica)

JAMAICA a
1:3 000 000
10 0 10 20 30 40 50 km
10 0 10 20 30 miles

CARIBBEAN SEA

Montego Bay
Lucea
Falmouth
Runaway Bay
St. Ann's Bay
Galina Point
Port Maria
Negril
South Negril Pt.
Wakefield
The Cockpit Country
Ocho Rios
Dry Harbour Mountains
Moneague
Annotto Bay
Port Antonio
Cambridge
Mount Denham 985
Savanna-la-Mar
Maggotty
Don Figuero Mts.
Linstead
Spanish Town
The Blue Mountains 2256
Blue Mt. Pk.
John Crow Mts.
Black River
Mandeville
Santa Cruz Mts.
May Pen
Portmore
Kingston
Morant Point
Port Antonio
Great Pedro Bluff
Alligator Pond
Portland Bight
Portland Point
Morant Bay
Port Morant

JAMAICA

0
200 600
2000 6000
4000 12 000
6000 18 000
m ft

b
Pte. de la Grande Vigie
Port-Louis
Grande-Terre
Petit-Canal
Pointe Allègre
Ste-Rose
Le Moule
La Désirade
Pointe-Noire
Pointe-à-Pitre
Ste-Anne
Pointe des Châteaux
Basse-Terre
Bouillante
Le Gosier
Îles de la Petite Terre
Soufrière 1467
Capesterre-Belle-Eau
Ste-Louis
Marie-Galante
Basse-Terre
Trois-Rivières
204
Capesterre
Îles des Saintes
Grand-Bourg
Pte. des Basses
GUADELOUPE (Fr.)

c
Cap St-Martin
Basse-Pointe
Le Prêcheur
Montagne Pelée 1397
Ste-Marie
Presqu'île de la Caravelle
St-Pierre
La Trinité
Le Robert
St-Joseph
Schœlcher
Le François
Fort-de-France
Le Lamentin
Rivière-Salée
Le St-Esprit
MARTINIQUE (Fr.)
Le Marin
Rivière-Pilote
Pte. d'Enfer

GUADELOUPE AND MARTINIQUE
1:2 000 000
10 0 10 20 30 40 km
10 0 10 20 30 miles

Projection : Bonne

6 **7**

PUERTO RICO d
1:3 000 000
10   0   10   20   30   40   50 km
10   0   10   20   30 miles

ATLANTIC OCEAN
67   66

PUERTO RICO
(U.S.A.)

Aguadilla   Isabela
Arecibo   Manati   Vega   Barceloneta   Rio Grande   SAN JUAN
Mayagüez   San   Baja   Bayamón   Carolina
               Sebastián   Utuado   Caguas   Sierra de   Fajardo   Dewey
                         Adjuntas   Córdillera Central   Cayey   Liquillo   Pta.   Culebra
San German   C. de Punta   Humacoa   Puerca   Vieques
               Yauco   1338   Naguabo   Esperanza
Pta. Aguila   Guanica   Ponce   Coamo   Yabucoa   Guayama
               I. Caja de Muertos

VIRGIN IS. e
1:2 000 000
10   0   10   20   30 km
10   0   10   20 miles

64° 30'
Rufling Pt.   The
              Settlement
Virgin Islands   Anegada   East
(U.K.)   Pt.

18° 30'   18° 30'
Jost Van   Great
Virgin Is.   Dyke I.   Camanoe
(U.S.A.)   Hans   Guana I.   Beef   Virgin Gorda
          Lollik I.   521   Tortola   Spanish Town
Charlotte   Cruz   Road Town   Peter I.
Amalie   Bay   St.   St. John I.
         St.   Thomas I.
65   64° 30'

ST. LUCIA f
1:1 000 000
5   0   10 km
5   0   5   10 miles

Cap Point   Pte. Hardy
Gros Islet   Esperance Bay
Castries   Marquis
           Girard
Anse la Raye
Canaries   Millet   Dennery
Soufrière   750   Trou Gras Pt.
Soufrière   Mt. Gimie
Bay   796   1950   Micoud
Petit Piton   Vierge Pt.
Gros Piton Pt.   Gros Piton
Choiseul   Laborie   Vieux Fort   ST. LUCIA
61   C. Moule à Chique

14   14

BARBADOS g
1:1 000 000
5   0   10 km
5   0   5   10 miles

59° 30'   ATLANTIC
Crab Hill   North Point   OCEAN
Fustic   Spring Hall
         Boscobelle
13° 15'   245   Belleplaine   13° 15'
Speightstown   Bathsheba   BARBADOS
Westmoreland   340   Hillcrest
Alleynes Bay   Mt. Hillaby   Martin's Bay
Holetown   Massiah
Jackson   Bridgefield   Street
Black Rock   Ellerton   Kitridge Pt.
         Six Cross Roads
Bridgetown   Oistins   The Crane
Carlisle Bay   St. Martins
Worthing   Oistins   Chancery Lane
         Bay   South Point
59° 30'

10   11   12   C

CUBA / CARIBBEAN MAP

ATLANTA   Columbia   Wilmington
Macon   Augusta   C. Fear
Columbus   Savannah   Long Bay
Charleston
Albany   C. Romain

Jacksonville
allahassee

ORLANDO   Daytona Beach
TAMPA   Melbourne
St. Petersburg   C. Canaveral
Sarasota   West Palm Beach
L. Okeechobee   Grand Bahama I.
MIAMI   Fort Lauderdale   Freeport   Abaco I.
C. Sable   Bimini Is.   New Providence I.   Eleuthera I.
Key West   Andros I.   Nassau   Cat I.
Straits of Florida   BAHAMAS   San Salvador I.

LA HABANA   Matanzas   Cárdenas   Great Exuma I.
(Havana)   Sagua la Grande   Long I.
el Rio   Guines   Santa Clara   Crooked I.
G. de   Cienfuegos   Placetos   Morón   Mayaguana I.
Batabanó   C U B A   Camagüey   Acklins
I. de la   Trinidad   Sancti Spíritus   Ciego de Ávila   Great Inagua
Juventud   G   Las Tunas   Nuevitas   Turks & Caicos Is.
r   e   Holguín   Banes   Cockburn
Grand   a   Bayamo   Baracoa   Town (U.K.)
Cayman   t   1972   Santiago   GUANTÁNAMO   Port-de-Paix
George Town   e   de Cuba   (U.S.A.)   Cap-Haïtien   Monte Christi   Puerto Plata
(U.K.)   r   Guantánamo   Gonaïves   Santiago de   San francisco
7680   Montego Bay   St-Marc   los Caballeros   de Macoris
Mandeville   Spanish Town   A   Jérémie   3175   La Vega
JAMAICA   Kingston   n   Les Cayes   San Juan   La Romana
              t   Jacmel   Barahona
              i   PORT-AU-PRINCE   SANTO DOMINGO
              l   HAITI   DOMINICAN   San Pedro
              l   Hispaniola   REP.   de Macoris
              e   PUERTO RICO
              s

CARIBBEAN SEA

L. de Caratasca
Coco   C. Gracias a Dios
iUA   Puerto Cabezas
Rio Grande   I. de Providencia (Colombia)
Bluefields   I. de San Andrés (Colombia)

olcan Irazú   COSTA RICA   Limón
3432   G. de los Mosquitos   Panama Canal
Cartago   Colón
ose   Volcán Barú   Panamá
Palmar   3475   P A N A M Á
Sur   David   Chitré   Arch. de las Perlas
Puerto   Santiago   La Palma   El Real
Armuelles   Pen. de   Jaque   Riosucio
I. de   Azuero   G. de   Pen. de
Coiba   Panamá

I. de Malpelo (Colombia)

Buenaventura   CALI   Palmira
              Huila   Neiva
              3750   Popayán
              Volcán Puracé   4646

9200   Puerto Rico Trench

Port-au-Prince Passage

Mona   Arecibo   SAN JUAN
Ponce   St. Croix   Virgin Is.   Anguilla (U.K.)
       (U.S.A.)   (U.S.A. - U.K.)   St-Martin (Fr. - Neth.)
Mona   Mayagüez   St-Barthélemy (Fr.)
       PUERTO RICO   ST. KITTS & NEVIS
       (U.S.A.)   Basseterre   ANTIGUA &
       Caguas   St. John's   BARBUDA
              Montserrat (U.K.)   GUADELOUPE (Fr.)
              Pointe-à-Pitre
              Leeward   Basse-Terre
              Islands   DOMINICA
       L e s s e r   Roseau

Fort-de-France   MARTINIQUE (Fr.)
A n t i l l e s   Castries
              ST. LUCIA
ST. VINCENT &   Kingstown   BARBADOS
THE GRENADINES   Bridgetown
              Windward
              Islands   GRENADA
              St. George's   Tobago
La Blanquilla (Ven.)

Pta. Gallinas
Aruba (Neth.)   Curaçao   Punto   Willemstad   Bonaire
Pen. de la   Fijo   NETH.
Guajira   ANTILLES   I. de Margarita   Port of Spain
              Porlamar   TRINIDAD & TOBAGO
Santa Marta   Ríohacha   Coro   Puerto   Cumaná   Güiria
BARRANQUILLA   San   Cabello   MARACAY   Carúpano   G. de
              Felipe   MARACAIBO   Maiquetía   Paria   San Fernando
Cartagena   Soledad   Cabimas   CARACAS   Puerto La
              Sierra Nevada   Valencia   Cruz   Barcelona
Calamar   de Santa Marta   L. de   VALENCIA
              5800   Maracaibo   Barquisimeto   El Tigre
Sincelejo   Valledupar   Valera   Acarigua
Mompós   Magdalena   Merida   Barinas   Apure   Orinoco   Ciudad
Monteria   5007   San Fernando   Guayana
Puerto Wilches   Cúcuta   San Cristóbal   de Apure   Ciudad Bolívar   Georgetown
Barrancabermeja   Pamplona   Arauca   Embalse de Guri   Bartica
2960   Yarumal   Bucaramanga   Caicara   Cuyuni   New Amsterdam
Antioquia   V E N E Z U E L A   Tumeremo   Linden
Bello   Sogamoso   Puerto Carreño   Mt. Roraima   Wismar
MEDELLÍN   Puerto Ayacucho   2772   G U Y A N A
Quibdó   Meta   Vichada   Caura
C. Corrientes   Tunja   C O L O M B I A   Sierra Pacaraima   SURINAME
Manizales   Villavicencio   Vaupés   Serra
Pereira   BOGOTÁ   Puerto Inírida   Parima
Armenia   Tolima   Ibagué   Orinoco   Boa Vista
5215   Girardot   Guaviare   Casiquiare
              Guainía

B R A Z I L
Equator

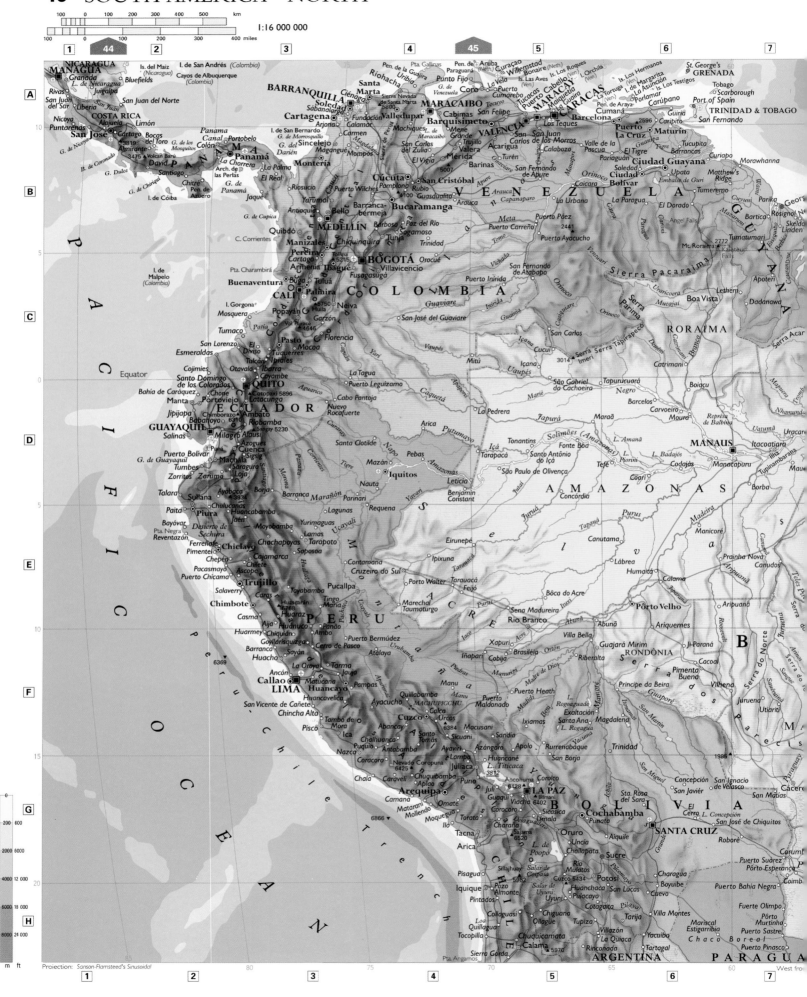

ATLANTIC

OCEAN

TRINIDAD AND
TOBAGO
1:2 500 000
10 0 10 20 30 40 50 km
10 0   10   20   30 miles

Tobago Castara Charlotteville North Pt.
Plymouth Main Ridge Little
Buccoo Reef Roxborough Tobago
Crown Pt. Scarborough Rocky Bay

VENEZUELA
Pen. de Macuro Corozal
Paria Monos Pt.
Dragon's Mouths
Güiria

La Vache Pt.
Maracas Bay
Chupara Pt.
Blanchisseuse
Maraval
Port San
of Juan
Spain
Caroni
Chaguanas

Sans Souci
Matelot
Toco
Galera Pt.
Redhead
Salybia
Northern Range
936 940 ▲Mt. Aripo
Tunapuna Valencia Matura
Arima Bay
Guaico Sangre Grande
Talparo Upper Manzanilla
Couva Nariva Cocos
Swamp Bay
Point Lisas ATLANTIC
Otaheite Bay Rio Claro Guataro Pt. OCEAN
Gasparillo
San Fernando Pierreville
Brighton Penal Mayaro Bay
Guapo Bay La Brea Trinidad
Point Fortin Pitch Princes Town Guayaguayare
Lake Basse Terre Galeota Pt.
Cedros Bay Palo Seco 304▲
Bonasse Siparia Trinity
Icacos Pt. Erin Pt. La Lune Moruga Hills

Golfo de Paria

Chaguanas

Serpent's Mouth
VENEZUELA Pta. Bombeder West from Greenwich

AMAPÁ

SURINAME FRENCH
GUIANA

BRAZIL

TO GROSSO Planalto do

MATO GROSSO

MATO GROSSO
DO SUL

GOIÁS

MINAS GERAIS

PARÁ

MARANHÃO

CEARÁ

PIAUÍ

TOCANTINS

BAHIA

PERNAMBUCO

PARAÍBA

RIO GRANDE
DO NORTE

FORTALEZA

Natal

RECIFE

Maceió

Aracaju

SALVADOR

BRASÍLIA

BELO HORIZONTE

RIO DE JANEIRO

CAMPINAS

SÃO PAULO

COPYRIGHT PHILIP'S

1:16 000 000

km
miles

Projection: Sanson-Flamsteed's Sinusoidal

West from Greenwich

COPYRIGHT PHILIP'S

PARAGUAY

ASUNCIÓN

BRAZIL

PARANÁ

SÃO PAULO

RIO DE JANEIRO

CAMPINAS

CURITIBA

SANTA CATARINA

Florianópolis

RIO GRANDE DO SUL

PÔRTO ALEGRE

URUGUAY

MONTEVIDEO

BUENOS AIRES

ROSARIO

CÓRDOBA

San Miguel de Tucumán

Santiago del Estero

MENDOZA

SANTIAGO

Valparaíso

Viña del Mar

Concepción

Talcahuano

Temuco

Valdivia

Osorno

Puerto Montt

La Plata

Mar del Plata

Bahía Blanca

Neuquén

Comodoro Rivadavia

ARGENTINA

CHILE

PATAGONIA

Tierra del Fuego

Ushuaia

Punta Arenas

Estrecho de Magallanes (Magellan's Str.)

Río Gallegos

C. de Hornos (C. Horn)

FALKLAND ISLANDS (ISLAS MALVINAS) (U.K.)
Stanley
West Falkland
East Falkland
Port Darwin

South Georgia (U.K.)

SOUTH ATLANTIC OCEAN

PACIFIC OCEAN

Peru–Chile Trench

Tropic of Capricorn

Chaco Boreal

INDEX

The index contains the names of all the principal places and features shown on the maps. The alphabetical order of names composed of two or more words is governed primarily by the first word and then by the second. This is an example of the rule:

Physical features composed of a proper name (Erie) and a description (Lake) are positioned alphabetically by the proper name. The description is positioned after the proper name and is usually abbreviated:

Where a description forms part of a settlement name or administrative name, however, it is always written in full and put in its true alphabetical position:

The number in bold type which follows each name in the index refers to the number of the map page where that place or feature will be found. This is usually the largest scale at which the place or feature appears.

The letter and figure which are immediately after the page number give the grid square on the map page, within which the feature is situated. The letter represents the latitude and the figure the longitude. In some cases the feature itself may fall within the specified square, while the name is outside.

Rivers are indexed to their mouths or confluences and carry the symbol → after their names. The following symbols are also used in the index: ■ country, ☑ overseas territory or dependency, □ first order administrative area, △ national park or reserve.

Gail 41 J4
Gainesville, *Fla.*, *U.S.A.* 43 L4
Gainesville, *Ga.*, *U.S.A.* 43 H4
Gainesville, *Mo.*, *U.S.A.* 41 G8
Gainesville, *Tex.*, *U.S.A.* 41 J6
Gainsborough 8 D7
Gairdner, L. 32 B2
Gairloch 10 D3
Gairloch, L. 10 D3
Galápagos = Colón, Arch. de 35 H18
Galapagos Fracture Zone 35 G17
Galapagos Rise 35 J18
Galashiels 10 F6
Galați 15 B13
Galax 43 G5
Galcaio 24 E3
Galdhøpiggen 7 E5
Galela 23 C4
Galena 36 C4
Galesburg 40 E9
Galicia □ 13 A2
Galina Pt. 44 a
Galiuro Mts. 39 K8
Gallan Hd. 10 C1
Gallatin 43 G2
Galle 25 E7
Galley Hd. 11 E3
Gallipoli = Gelibolu 15 D12
Gallipolis 42 F4
Gällivare 7 D8
Galloway 10 F4
Galloway △ 10 F4
Galloway, Mull of 10 G4
Gallup 39 J9
Galty Mts. 11 D3
Galtymore 11 D3
Galva 40 E9
Galveston 41 L7
Galveston B. 41 L7
Galway 11 C2
Galway □ 11 C2
Galway B. 11 C2
Gambia ■ 26 F2
Gambia → 26 F2
Gambier, Îs. 35 K14
Gambier Is. 32 C2
Gammon Ranges △ 32 B2
Gan Jiang → 21 D6
Ganado 39 J9
Gäncä 17 B7
Gander 37 E14
Ganga → 25 C8
Ganges = Ganga → 25 C8
Gani 23 D4
Gannett Peak 38 E9
Gansu □ 20 C5
Gantheaume, C. 32 C2
Ganzhou 21 D6
Gao 26 E5
Gap 12 D7
Gar 20 C2
Gara, L. 11 C3
Garagum 18 F6
Garah 32 A4
Garberville 38 F2
Garda, L. di 14 B4
Garden City, *Ga.*, *U.S.A.* 43 J5
Garden City, *Kans.*, *U.S.A.* 41 G4
Garden City, *Tex.*, *U.S.A.* 41 K4
Gardēz 25 B5
Gardiner, *Maine*, *U.S.A.* 43 C11
Gardiner, *Mont.*, *U.S.A.* 38 D8
Gardnerville 38 G4
Gardo 24 E3
Garfield 38 C5
Garforth 8 D6
Gargantua, C. 42 B3
Garland, *Tex.*, *U.S.A.* 41 J6
Garland, *Utah*, *U.S.A.* 38 F7
Garner 40 D8
Garnett 40 F7
Garoe 24 E3
Garonne → 12 D3
Garrison, *Mont.*, *U.S.A.* 38 C7
Garrison, *N. Dak.*, *U.S.A.* 40 B4
Garron Pt. 11 A6
Garry → 10 E5
Garry, L. 36 C9
Garstang 8 D5
Garvie Mts. 33 L2
Gary 42 E2
Garzê 20 C5
Gascogne 12 E4
Gascogne, G. de 12 D2
Gaspé 37 E13
Gaspésie, Pén. de la 37 E13
Gastonia 43 H5
Gatehouse of Fleet 10 G4
Gateshead 8 C6
Gatesville 41 K6
Gatineau 42 C8
Gatton 32 A5
Gatwick, London (LGW) 9 F7
Gau 33 D8
Gaua 31 C12
Gävle 7 E7
Gawler 32 B2
Gaxun Nur 20 B5
Gaya 25 C7
Gaylord 42 C3
Gayndah 32 A5
Gaza 17 D4
Gaza Strip ■ 24 B2
Gaziantep 17 C5
Gcuwa 29 L5
Gdańsk 16 A9
Gdańska, Zatoka 16 A9
Gdynia 16 A9
Gebe 23 C4
Gedser 7 G6
Geelong 32 C3
Gejiu 20 D5
Gelib 24 E3
Gelibolu 15 D12
Gelsenkirchen 16 C3
General Santos 23 C4
Genesee 38 C5
Genesee → 42 D7
Geneseo, *Ill.*, *U.S.A.* 40 E9
Geneseo, *N.Y.*, *U.S.A.* 42 D7
Geneva = Genève 12 C7
Geneva, *Ala.*, *U.S.A.* 43 K3
Geneva, *N.Y.*, *U.S.A.* 42 D7
Geneva, *Nebr.*, *U.S.A.* 40 E6
Geneva, *Ohio*, *U.S.A.* 42 E5
Genève 12 C7
Gennargentu, Mti. del 14 D3
Genoa = Génova 12 D8
Genoa, *Australia* 32 C4
Genoa, *U.S.A.* 40 E6
Génova 12 D8
Gent 16 C1
George 29 L4
George → 37 D13
George, L., *N.S.W., Australia* 32 C4
George, L., *S. Austral.*, *Australia* 32 C3
George, L., *Fla.*, *U.S.A.* 43 L5
George, L., *N.Y.*, *U.S.A.* 42 D9
George Sound 33 L1
George Town, *Australia* 32 D4
George Town, *Malaysia* 23 C2
George V Land 6 D14
George West 41 L5
Georgetown, *Guyana* 46 B7
Georgetown, *Colo.*, *U.S.A.* 38 G11
Georgetown, *Ky.*, *U.S.A.* 42 F3
Georgetown, *Ohio*, *U.S.A.* 42 F4
Georgetown, *S.C.*, *U.S.A.* 43 J6
Georgetown, *Tex.*, *U.S.A.* 41 K6
Georgia □ 43 K5
Georgian B. 37 E11
Gera 16 C6
Geraldine 38 C8
Geraldton 30 F1
Gereshk 24 B5
Gering 40 E3
Gerlach 38 F4
Germantown 41 M10
Germany ■ 16 C5
Germiston 29 K5
Gerona = Girona 13 B7
Getafe 13 B4
Gettysburg, *Pa.*, *U.S.A.* 42 F7
Gettysburg, *S. Dak.*, *U.S.A.* 40 C5
Geyser 38 C8
Ghana ■ 26 G5
Ghanzi 29 J4
Ghats, Eastern 25 D6
Ghats, Western 25 D6
Ghazâl, Bahr el → 27 G12
Ghaziabad 25 C6
Ghaznī 24 B5
Ghent = Gent 16 C1
Giant Sequoia △ 39 J4
Giants Causeway 11 A5
Gibbon 40 E5
Gibraltar ⧄ 13 D3
Gibraltar, Str. of 13 E3
Gibraltar Range △ 32 A5
Gibson Desert 30 E4
Giddings 41 K6
Gifu 22 F5
Gigha 10 F3
Gijón 13 A3
Gila → 39 K6
Gila Bend 39 K7
Gila Bend Mts. 39 K7
Gila Cliff Dwellings △ 39 K9
Gilbert Is. 31 A14
Gilgandra 32 B4
Gilgit 25 B6
Gillam 36 D10
Gilles, L. 32 B2
Gillette 40 C2
Gillingham 9 F8
Gilmer 41 J7
Gilroy 39 H3
Gimie, Mt 45 f
Gin Gin 32 A5
Giohar 24 E3
Girard 41 G7
Girdle Ness 10 D6
Girona 13 B7
Gironde → 12 D3
Girraween △ 32 A5
Girvan 10 F4
Gisborne 33 H7
Giuba → 24 E3
Giza = El Giza 27 C12
Gizhiga 19 C17
Gjoa Haven 36 C10
Glace Bay 37 E14
Glacier △ 38 B7
Glacier Peak 38 B3
Gladewater 41 J7
Gladstone, *Queens.*, *Australia* 30 E9
Gladstone, *S. Austral.*, *Australia* 32 B2
Gladstone, *U.S.A.* 42 C2
Gladwin 42 D3
Glamorgan, Vale of □ 9 F4
Glasco 40 F6
Glasgow, *U.K.* 10 F4
Glasgow, *Ky.*, *U.S.A.* 42 G3
Glasgow, *Mont.*, *U.S.A.* 38 B10
Glasgow Int. (GLA) 10 F4
Glastonbury 9 F5
Glen Affric 10 D3
Glen Canyon 39 H8
Glen Canyon △ 39 H8
Glen Canyon Dam 39 H8
Glen Coe 10 E3
Glen Garry 10 D3
Glen Innes 32 A5
Glen Mor 10 D4
Glen More △ 10 D5
Glen Moriston 10 D4
Glen Spean 10 E4
Glen Ullin 40 B4
Glenallen 36 C5
Glenariff △ 11 A5
Glenbeigh 11 D2
Glencoe 40 C7
Glencolumbkille 11 B3
Glendale, *Ariz.*, *U.S.A.* 39 K7
Glendale, *Calif.*, *U.S.A.* 39 J4
Glendive 40 B2
Glendo 40 D2
Glenelg → 32 C3
Glengad Hd. 11 A4
Glengarriff 11 E2
Glenmorgan 32 A4
Glennamaddy 11 C3
Glenns Ferry 38 E6
Glenreagh 32 B5
Glenrock 38 E11
Glenrothes 10 E5
Glens Falls 42 D9
Glenties 11 B3
Glenveagh △ 11 A3
Glenville 42 F5
Glenwood, *Ark.*, *U.S.A.* 41 H8
Glenwood, *Iowa*, *U.S.A.* 40 E7
Glenwood, *Minn.*, *U.S.A.* 40 C7
Glenwood Springs 38 G10
Glin 11 D2
Gliwice 16 C9
Globe 39 K8
Głogów 16 C8
Glomma → 7 F6
Glossop 8 D6
Gloucester, *Australia* 32 B5
Gloucester, *U.K.* 9 F5
Gloucester Point 42 G7
Gloucestershire □ 9 F5
Gniezno 16 B8
Goa □ 25 D6
Goalen Hd. 32 C5
Goat Fell 10 F3
Gobabis 29 J3
Gobi 21 B5
Godalming 9 F7
Godavari → 25 D7
Gods → 36 D10
Gods L. 36 D10
Gogebic, L. 40 B10
Goiânia 47 G9
Goio-Erê 48 A6
Golconda 38 F5
Gold Beach 38 E1
Gold Coast, *Australia* 30 F9
Gold Coast, *W. Afr.* 26 H5
Gold Hill 38 E2
Golden B. 33 J4
Golden Gate 38 H2
Golden Spike △ 38 F7
Golden Vale 11 D3
Goldendale 38 D3
Goldfield 39 H5
Goldsboro 43 H7
Goldsmith 41 K3
Goldthwaite 41 K5
Goliad 41 L6
Golspie 10 D5
Gómez Palacio 44 B4
Gonābād 24 B4
Gonaïves 45 D10
Gongbei 21 G10
Gongga Shan 25 C9
Gonghe 20 C5
Gongming 21 F10
Gongolgon 32 B4
Gonzales, *Calif.*, *U.S.A.* 39 H3
Gonzales, *Tex.*, *U.S.A.* 41 L6
Good Hope, C. of 29 L3
Gooding 38 E6
Goodland 40 F4
Goodooga 32 A4
Goole 8 D7
Goolgowi 32 B4
Goomeri 32 A5
Goondiwindi 32 A5
Goose Creek 43 J5
Goose L. 38 F3
Gorakhpur 25 C7
Gordon 40 D3
Gordon → 32 D4
Gore 33 M2
Gorey 11 D5
Gorgān 24 B4
Gorleston 9 E9
Görlitz 16 C7
Gorontalo 23 C4
Gort 11 C3
Gorzów Wielkopolski 16 B7
Gosford 32 B5
Goshen 42 E3
Gosport 9 G6
Göta kanal 7 F7
Göteborg 7 F6
Gotha 16 C5
Gothenburg = Göteborg 7 F6
Gothenburg 40 E4
Gotland 7 F7
Göttingen 16 C4
Gouda 16 B2
Gouin, Rés. 37 E12
Goulburn 32 B4
Gourock 10 F4
Gouverneur 42 C8
Governador Valadares 47 G10
Gowanda 42 D6
Gower 9 F3
Gowna, L. 11 C4
Goyder Lagoon 32 A2
Gozo 14 F6
Graaff-Reinet 29 L4
Gracias a Dios, C. 45 E8
Grady 41 H3
Grafham Water 9 E7
Grafton, *Australia* 32 A5
Grafton, *N. Dak.*, *U.S.A.* 40 A6
Grafton, *W. Va.*, *U.S.A.* 42 F5
Graham 41 J5
Graham, Mt. 39 K9
Graham Land 6 D3
Grahamstown 29 L5
Grain Coast 26 H3
Grampian Mts. 10 E5
Grampians, The 32 C3
Gran Canaria 26 C2
Gran Chaco 48 B4
Gran Sasso d'Itália 14 C5
Granada, *Nic.* 44 E7
Granada, *Spain* 13 D4
Granada, *U.S.A.* 41 F3
Granard 11 C4
Granbury 41 J6
Granby, *Canada* 37 E12
Granby, *U.S.A.* 38 F11
Grand →, *Mo.*, *U.S.A.* 40 F8
Grand →, *S. Dak.*, *U.S.A.* 40 C4
Grand Bahama I. 45 B9
Grand-Bourg 44 b
Grand Canyon 39 H7
Grand Canyon △ 39 H7
Grand Canyon-Parashant △ 39 H7
Grand Cayman 45 D8
Grand Coulee 38 C4
Grand Coulee Dam 38 C4
Grand Falls 37 E13
Grand Falls-Windsor 37 E14
Grand Forks 40 B6
Grand Haven 42 D2
Grand I. 42 B2
Grand Island 40 E5
Grand Isle 41 L9
Grand Junction 39 G9
Grand L. 41 L8
Grand Lake 38 F11
Grand Marais 42 B3
Grand Portage 40 B10
Grand Prairie 41 J6
Grand Rapids, *Canada* 36 D10
Grand Rapids, *Mich.*, *U.S.A.* 42 D2
Grand Rapids, *Minn.*, *U.S.A.* 40 B8
Grand St-Bernard, Col du 12 D7
Grand Staircase-Escalante △ 39 H8
Grand Teton 38 E8
Grand Teton △ 38 D8
Grand Union Canal 9 E7
Grand-Vigie, Pte. de la 44 b
Grande, Rio → 41 N6
Grande Baleine, R. de la → 37 D12
Grande Prairie 36 D8
Grande-Terre 44 b
Grandfalls 41 K3
Grandview 38 C4
Grangemouth 10 E5
Granger 38 F9
Grangeville 38 D5
Granite City 40 F9
Granite Falls 40 C7
Granite Pk. 38 D9
Granity 33 J3
Grant 40 E4
Grant, Mt. 38 G4
Grant City 40 E7
Grant Range 39 G6
Grantham 8 E7
Grantown-on-Spey 10 D5
Grants 39 J10
Grants Pass 38 E2
Grantsville 38 F7
Granville, *N. Dak.*, *U.S.A.* 40 A4
Granville, *N.Y.*, *U.S.A.* 42 D9
Grass Range 38 C9
Grass Valley, *Calif.*, *U.S.A.* 38 G3
Grass Valley, *Oreg.*, *U.S.A.* 38 D3
Grasse 12 E7
Grassy 32 D3
Graulhet 12 E4
's-Gravenhage 16 B2
Gravesend, *Australia* 32 A5
Gravesend, *U.K.* 9 F8
Grayling 42 C3
Grays 9 F8
Grays Harbor 38 C1
Grays L. 38 E8
Graz 16 E7
Great Australian Bight 30 G5
Great Bahama Bank 44 B4
Great Barrier I. 33 G5
Great Barrier Reef 30 D8
Great Basin 38 G5
Great Basin △ 38 G6
Great Bear → 36 C7
Great Bear L. 36 C8
Great Bend 40 F5
Great Blasket I. 11 D1
Great Camanoe 45 e
Great Channel 25 E8
Great Dividing Ra. 30 E8
Great Exuma I. 45 C9
Great Falls 38 C8
Great Inagua I. 45 C10
Great Karoo 29 L4
Great Lake 32 D4
Great Malvern 9 E5
Great Miami → 42 F3
Great Ormes Head 8 D4
Great Ouse → 8 E8
Great Pedro Bluff 44 a
Great Pee Dee → 43 J6
Great Plains 2 C5
Great Salt L. 38 F7
Great Salt Lake Desert 38 F7
Great Salt Plains L. 41 G5
Great Sand Dunes △ 39 H11
Great Sandy △ 32 A5
Great Sandy Desert 30 E3
Great Skellig 11 E1
Great Slave L. 36 C8
Great Smoky Mts. △ 43 H4
Great Snow Mt. 36 D7
Great Victoria Desert 30 F4
Great Wall 21 C5
Great Whernside 8 C6
Great Yarmouth 9 E9
Greater Antilles 45 D10
Greater London □ 9 F7
Greater Manchester □ 8 D5
Greater Sunda Is. 23 D3
Greece ■ 15 E9
Greeley, *Colo.*, *U.S.A.* 40 E2
Greeley, *Nebr.*, *U.S.A.* 40 E5
Greely Fd. 37 B10
Greem-Bell, Ostrov 18 A7
Green →, *Ky.*, *U.S.A.* 42 G2
Green →, *Utah*, *U.S.A.* 39 G9
Green B. 42 C2
Green Bay 42 C2
Green C. 32 C5
Green Cove Springs 43 L5
Green River, *Utah*, *U.S.A.* 39 G8
Green River, *Wyo.*, *U.S.A.* 38 F9
Green Valley 39 L8
Greenbush 40 A6
Greencastle 42 F2
Greeneville 43 G4
Greenfield, *Ind.*, *U.S.A.* 42 F3
Greenfield, *Iowa*, *U.S.A.* 40 E7
Greenfield, *Mass.*, *U.S.A.* 42 D9
Greenfield, *Mo.*, *U.S.A.* 41 G8
Greenland ⧄ 6 C4
Greenland Sea 6 B6
Greenock 10 F4
Greenore 11 B5
Greenore Pt. 11 D5
Greensboro, *Ga.*, *U.S.A.* 43 J4
Greensboro, *N.C.*, *U.S.A.* 43 G6
Greensburg, *Ind.*, *U.S.A.* 42 F3
Greensburg, *Kans.*, *U.S.A.* 41 G5
Greensburg, *Pa.*, *U.S.A.* 42 E6
Greenstone Pt. 10 D3
Greenville, *Ala.*, *U.S.A.* 43 K2
Greenville, *Calif.*, *U.S.A.* 38 F3
Greenville, *Maine*, *U.S.A.* 43 C11
Greenville, *Mich.*, *U.S.A.* 42 D3
Greenville, *Miss.*, *U.S.A.* 41 J9
Greenville, *Mo.*, *U.S.A.* 41 G9
Greenville, *N.C.*, *U.S.A.* 43 H7
Greenville, *Ohio*, *U.S.A.* 42 E3
Greenville, *Pa.*, *U.S.A.* 42 E5
Greenville, *S.C.*, *U.S.A.* 43 H4
Greenville, *Tex.*, *U.S.A.* 41 J6
Greenwich □ 9 F8
Greenwood, *Ark.*, *U.S.A.* 41 H7
Greenwood, *Ind.*, *U.S.A.* 42 F2
Greenwood, *Miss.*, *U.S.A.* 41 J9
Greenwood, *S.C.*, *U.S.A.* 43 H4
Gregory 40 D5
Gregory, L. 32 A2
Grenada 41 J10
Grenada ■ 45 E12
Grenfell 32 B4
Grenoble 12 D6
Gresham 38 D2
Gretna, *U.K.* 10 F5
Gretna, *U.S.A.* 41 L9
Grey → 33 K3
Grey Ra. 32 A3
Greybull 38 D9
Greymouth 33 K3
Greystones 11 C5
Greytown 33 J5
Gridley 38 G3
Griffin 43 J3
Griffith 32 B4
Grimsay 10 D1
Grimsby 8 D7
Grinnell 40 E8
Gris-Nez, C. 12 A4
Grise Fiord 37 B10
Groesbeck 41 K6
Groningen 16 B3
Groom 41 H4
Groote Eylandt 30 C6
Gros Islet 45 f
Gros Piton 45 f
Gros Piton Pt. 45 f
Grossglockner 16 E6
Groton 40 C5
Grove Hill 43 K2
Groves 41 L8
Groveton 42 C10
Groznyy 17 B7
Grudziądz 16 B9
Gruinard B. 10 D3
Grundy Center 40 D8
Gruver 41 G4
Guadalajara, *Mexico* 44 C4
Guadalajara, *Spain* 13 B4
Guadalcanal 31 B11
Guadalete → 13 D2
Guadalquivir → 13 D2
Guadalupe 39 J3
Guadalupe → 41 L6
Guadalupe Mts. △ 41 K2
Guadalupe Peak 41 K2
Guadarrama, Sierra de 13 B4
Guadeloupe ⧄ 44 b
Guadiana → 13 D2
Guadix 13 D4
Guam ⧄ 34 F6
Guamúchil 44 B3
Guana I. 45 e
Guanajuato 44 C4
Guane 45 C8
Guangdong □ 21 D6
Guangxi Zhuangzu Zizhiqu □ 21 D5
Guangyuan 25 B9
Guangzhou 21 D6
Guanica 45 d
Guantánamo 45 C9
Guaporé → 46 F5
Guarapuava 48 B6
Guatemala 44 E6
Guatemala ■ 44 D6
Guatemala Basin 35 F18
Guatemala Trench 35 F18
Guaviare → 46 C5
Guayama 45 d
Guayaquil 46 D3
Guayaquil, G. de 46 D2
Guaymas 44 B2
Guéret 12 C4
Guernsey, *U.K.* 9 H5
Guernsey, *U.S.A.* 40 D2
Guildford 9 F7
Guilin 21 D6
Guinea ■ 26 F3
Guinea, Gulf of 4 D10
Guinea-Bissau ■ 26 F3
Güines 45 C8
Guingamp 12 B2
Guiyang 20 D5
Guizhou □ 20 D5
Gujarat □ 25 C6
Gujranwala 25 C6
Gulbarga 25 D6
Gulf Islands △ 43 E2
Gulfport 41 K10
Gulgong 32 B4
Gunnbjørn Fjeld 6 C5
Gunnedah 32 B5
Gunnewin 32 A4
Gunningbar Cr. → 32 B4
Gunnison, *Colo.*, *U.S.A.* 39 G10
Gunnison, *Utah*, *U.S.A.* 38 G8
Gunnison → 39 G9
Guntersville 43 H2
Guntur 25 D7
Gurdon 41 J8
Gurley 32 A4
Gusinoozersk 19 D11
Gustine 39 H3
Guthrie, *Okla.*, *U.S.A.* 41 H6
Guthrie, *Tex.*, *U.S.A.* 41 J4
Guttenberg 40 D9
Guwahati 20 D4
Guy Fawkes River △ 32 A5
Guyana ■ 46 C7
Guyenne 12 D4
Guymon 41 G4
Guyra 32 B5
Gwabegar 32 B4
Gwādar 24 C5
Gwalior 25 C6
Gwangju 21 C7
Gweebarra B. 11 B3
Gweedore 11 A3
Gweru 29 H5
Gwinn 42 B2
Gwydir → 32 A4
Gwynedd □ 8 E3
Gyaring Hu 20 C4
Gympie 32 A5
Győr 16 E8
Gyumri 17 B6

H

Ha Tinh 23 B2
Ha'apai Group 31 D16
Haarlem 16 B2
Haast → 33 K2
Hachinohe 22 C7
Ḥadd, Ra's al 24 C4
Haddington 10 F6
Haḍramawt 24 D3
Hadrian's Wall 8 B5
Haeju 21 C7
Hafar al Bāṭin 24 C3
Hagen 16 C3
Hagerman 41 J2
Hagerman Fossil Beds △ 38 E6
Hagerstown 42 F7
Hagondange 12 B7
Hags Hd. 11 D2
Hague, C. de la 12 B3
Hague, The = 's-Gravenhage 16 B2
Haguenau 12 B7
Haifa = Ḥefa 17 D5
Haikou 21 D6
Ḥā'il 24 C3
Hailar 21 B6
Hailey 38 E6
Hainan □ 21 E5
Haines 38 D5
Haines City 43 L5
Haines Junction 36 C6
Haiphong 20 D5
Haiti ■ 45 D10
Ḥajjah 24 D3
Hakodate 22 C7
Ḥalab 24 B2
Halberstadt 16 C5
Halcombe 33 J5
Halden 7 F6
Halesowen 9 E5
Halesworth 9 E9
Haleyville 43 H2
Halfmoon Bay 33 M2
Halifax, *Canada* 37 E13
Halifax, *U.K.* 8 D6
Halīl → 24 C4
Halkirk 10 C5
Hall Pen. 37 C13
Hallāniyat, Jazā'ir al 24 D4
Halle 16 C5
Hallett 32 B2
Hallettsville 41 L6
Hallock 40 A6
Halls Creek 30 D4
Halmahera 23 C4
Halmstad 7 F6
Halstead 9 F8
Halton □ 8 D5
Haltwhistle 8 C5
Hamadān 24 B3
Ḥamāh 24 B2
Hamamatsu 22 F5
Hamar 7 E6
Hamburg, *Germany* 16 B4
Hamburg, *Ark.*, *U.S.A.* 41 J9
Hamburg, *N.Y.*, *U.S.A.* 42 D6
Hämeenlinna 7 E8
Hameln 16 B4
Hamersley Ra. 30 E2
Hami 20 B4
Hamilton, *Australia* 32 C3
Hamilton, *Canada* 37 E12
Hamilton, *N.Z.* 33 G5
Hamilton, *U.K.* 10 F4
Hamilton, *Ala.*, *U.S.A.* 43 H1
Hamilton, *Mont.*, *U.S.A.* 38 C6
Hamilton, *N.Y.*, *U.S.A.* 42 D8
Hamilton, *Ohio*, *U.S.A.* 42 F3
Hamilton, *Tex.*, *U.S.A.* 41 K5
Hamilton → 32 A2
Hamlet 43 H6
Hamley Bridge 32 B2
Hamlin 41 J4
Hamm 16 C3
Hammerfest 7 C8
Hammond, *Ind.*, *U.S.A.* 42 E2
Hammond, *La.*, *U.S.A.* 41 K9
Hammonton 42 F8
Hampden 33 L3
Hampshire □ 9 F6
Hampshire Downs 9 F6
Hampton, *Ark.*, *U.S.A.* 41 J8
Hampton, *Iowa*, *U.S.A.* 40 D8
Hampton, *S.C.*, *U.S.A.* 43 J5
Hampton, *Va.*, *U.S.A.* 42 G7
Hancock 40 B10
Handan 21 C6
Hanford 39 H4
Hanford Reach △ 38 C4
Hangayn Nuruu 20 B4
Hangzhou 21 C7
Hangzhou Wan 21 C7
Hankinson 40 B6
Hankö 7 F8
Hanksville 39 G8
Hanmer Springs 33 K4
Hanna, *Canada* 36 D8
Hanna, *U.S.A.* 38 F10
Hannibal 40 F9
Hannover 16 B4
Hanoi 20 D5
Hanover, *N.H.*, *U.S.A.* 42 D9
Hanover, *Pa.*, *U.S.A.* 42 F7
Hans Lollik I. 45 e
Hanson, L. 32 B2
Hanzhong 20 C5
Haora 25 C7
Haparanda 7 D8
Happy 41 H4
Happy Camp 38 F2
Happy Valley-Goose Bay 37 D13
Har Hu 20 C4
Har Us Nuur 20 B4
Ḥaraḍ 24 C3
Harare 29 H6
Harbin 21 B7
Harbor Beach 42 D4
Hardangerfjorden 7 E5
Hardin 38 D10
Hardy, Pte. 45 f
Harer 24 E3
Hargeisa 24 E3
Hari → 23 D2
Haridwar 25 C6
Harīrūd → 24 B5
Harlan, *Iowa*, *U.S.A.* 40 E7
Harlan, *Ky.*, *U.S.A.* 43 G4
Harlech 8 E3
Harlem 38 B9
Harlingen 41 M6
Harlow 9 F8
Harlowton 38 C9
Harney Basin 38 E4
Harney L. 38 E4
Harney Peak 40 D3
Härnösand 7 E7
Haroldswick 10 A8
Harricana → 37 D12
Harriman 43 H3
Harris 10 D2
Harris, L. 32 B2
Harris, Sd. of 10 D1
Harrisburg, *Ill.*, *U.S.A.* 41 G10
Harrisburg, *Nebr.*, *U.S.A.* 40 E3
Harrisburg, *Pa.*, *U.S.A.* 42 E7
Harrison, *Ark.*, *U.S.A.* 41 G8
Harrison, *Nebr.*, *U.S.A.* 40 D3
Harrison, C. 37 D14
Harrisonburg 42 F6
Harrisonville 40 F7
Harrisville 42 C4
Harrodsburg 42 G3
Harrogate 8 C6
Harrow □ 9 F7
Harry S. Truman Res. 40 F7
Hart 42 D2
Hart, L. 32 B2
Hartford, *Conn.*, *U.S.A.* 42 E9
Hartford, *Ky.*, *U.S.A.* 42 G2
Hartford, *S. Dak.*, *U.S.A.* 40 D6
Hartford, *Wis.*, *U.S.A.* 40 D10
Hartford City 42 E3
Hartland Pt. 9 F3
Hartlepool 8 C6
Hartselle 43 H2
Hartshorne 41 H7
Hartsville 43 H5
Hartwell 43 H4
Harvey, *Ill.*, *U.S.A.* 42 E2
Harvey, *N. Dak.*, *U.S.A.* 40 B5
Harwich 9 F9
Haryana □ 25 C6
Harz 16 C5
Hasa 24 C3
Haskell 41 J5
Haslemere 9 F7
Hastings, *N.Z.* 33 H6
Hastings, *U.K.* 9 G8
Hastings, *Mich.*, *U.S.A.* 42 D3
Hastings, *Minn.*, *U.S.A.* 40 C8
Hastings, *Nebr.*, *U.S.A.* 40 E5
Hastings Ra. 32 B5
Hat Yai 23 C2
Hatay 17 C4
Hatch 39 K10
Hatfield P.O. 32 B3
Hatgal 20 A5
Hattah 32 B3
Hatteras, C. 43 H8
Hattiesburg 41 K10
Haugesund 7 F5
Hauraki G. 33 G5
Haut Atlas 26 B4
Havana = La Habana 44 B3
Havana 40 E9
Havant 9 G7
Havasu, L. 39 J6
Havel → 16 B6
Havelock, *N.Z.* 33 J4
Havelock, *U.S.A.* 43 H7
Haverfordwest 9 F3
Haverhill, *U.K.* 9 E8
Haverhill, *U.S.A.* 42 D10
Havre 38 B9
Havre-St.-Pierre 37 D13
Haw → 43 H6
Hawaiian Is. 35 E12
Hawaiian Ridge 35 E11
Hawarden 40 D6
Hawea, L. 33 L2
Hawera 33 H5
Hawick 10 F6
Hawke B. 33 H6
Hawker 32 B2
Hawkinsville 43 J4
Hawley 40 B6
Hawthorne 38 G4
Hay 32 B3
Hay → 36 C8
Hay-on-Wye 9 E4
Hay River 36 C8
Hay Springs 40 D3
Hayden 38 F10
Hayes 40 C4
Hayes → 36 D10
Hayle 9 G2
Hayling I. 9 G7
Haymā' 24 D4
Hays 40 F5
Hayward, *Calif.*, *U.S.A.* 39 G2
Hayward, *Wis.*, *U.S.A.* 40 B9
Haywards Heath 9 G7
Hazard 42 G4
Hazelton 40 B4
Hazen 40 B4
Hazlehurst, *Ga.*, *U.S.A.* 43 K4
Hazlehurst, *Miss.*, *U.S.A.* 41 K9
Hazleton 42 E8
Healdsburg 38 G2
Healdton 41 H6
Healesville 32 C4
Heard I. 5 G14
Hearne 41 K6
Hearst 37 E11
Heart → 40 B4
Heathrow, London (LHR) 9 F7
Heavener 41 H7
Hebbronville 41 M5
Hebei □ 21 C6
Hebel 32 A4
Heber Springs 41 H9
Hebgen L. 38 D8
Hebrides, Sea of the 10 D2
Hebron, *Canada* 37 D13
Hebron, *N. Dak.*, *U.S.A.* 40 B3
Hebron, *Nebr.*, *U.S.A.* 40 E6
Hecate Str. 36 D6
Hechi 20 D5
Hechuan 20 C5
Hecla 40 C5
Heerlen 12 A6
Ḥefa 17 D5
Hefei 21 C6
Hegang 21 B8
Hei Ling Chau 21 G11
Heidelberg 16 D4
Heilbronn 16 D4
Heilongjiang □ 21 B7
Hejaz = Ḥijāz 24 C3
Hekou 20 D5
Helena, *Ark.*, *U.S.A.* 41 H9
Helena, *Mont.*, *U.S.A.* 38 C7
Helensburgh 10 E4
Helensville 33 G5
Helgoland 16 A3
Hells Canyon △ 38 D5
Helmand → 24 B5
Helmsdale 10 C5
Helmsdale → 10 C5
Helper 38 G8
Helsingborg 7 F6
Helsinki 7 E9
Helston 9 G2
Helvellyn 8 C4
Hemel Hempstead 9 F7
Hemet 39 K5
Hemingford 40 D3
Hempstead 41 K6
Henan □ 21 C6
Henderson, *Ky.*, *U.S.A.* 42 G2
Henderson, *N.C.*, *U.S.A.* 43 G6
Henderson, *Nev.*, *U.S.A.* 39 H6
Henderson, *Tenn.*, *U.S.A.* 43 H1
Henderson, *Tex.*, *U.S.A.* 41 J7
Henderson I. 35 K15
Hendersonville, *N.C.*, *U.S.A.* 43 H4
Hendersonville, *Tenn.*, *U.S.A.* 43 G2
Henggang 21 F11
Hengmen 21 F10
Hengqin Dao 21 G10
Hengyang 21 D6
Henley-on-Thames 9 F7
Henlopen, C. 42 F8
Hennessey 41 G6
Henrietta 41 J5
Henrietta Maria, C. 37 D11
Henry 40 E10
Henryetta 41 H7
Hentiyn Nuruu 21 B5
Henty 32 C4
Henzada 25 D8
Heppner 38 D4
Herāt 24 B5
Hereford, *U.K.* 9 E5
Hereford, *U.S.A.* 41 H3
Herefordshire □ 9 E5
Herford 16 B4
Herington 40 F6
Herkimer 42 D8
Herm 9 H5
Hermann 40 F9
Hermidale 32 B4
Hermiston 38 D4
Hermosillo 44 B2
Hernando 41 H10
Herne Bay 9 F9
Herreid 40 C4
Herrin 41 G10
Hertford 9 F7
Hertfordshire □ 9 F7
's-Hertogenbosch 16 C2
Hesperia 39 J5
Hessen □ 16 C4
Hettinger 40 C3
Hewitt 41 K6
Hexham 8 C5
Heysham 8 C5
Heywood 32 C3
Hialeah 43 N5
Hiawatha 40 F7
Hibbing 40 B8
Hibbs B. 32 D4
Hickman 41 G10
Hickory 43 H5
Hicks, Pt. 32 C4
Hidalgo del Parral 44 B3
Higashiōsaka 22 F4
Higgins 41 G4
High Island Res. 21 G11
High Level 36 D8
High Point 43 H6
High Prairie 36 D8
High River 36 D8
High Wycombe 9 F7
Highland □ 10 D4
Highland Park 42 D2
Highmore 40 C5
Ḥijāz 24 C3
Hiko 39 H6
Hikurangi, *Gisborne, N.Z.* 33 H6
Hikurangi, *Northland, N.Z.* 33 F5
Hildesheim 16 B4
Hill City, *Idaho*, *U.S.A.* 38 E6
Hill City, *Kans.*, *U.S.A.* 40 F5
Hill City, *Minn.*, *U.S.A.* 40 B8
Hill City, *S. Dak.*, *U.S.A.* 40 D3
Hillaby, Mt. 45 g
Hillcrest 45 g
Hillsboro, *Kans.*, *U.S.A.* 40 F6
Hillsboro, *N. Dak.*, *U.S.A.* 40 B6
Hillsboro, *Ohio*, *U.S.A.* 42 F4
Hillsboro, *Tex.*, *U.S.A.* 41 J6
Hillsborough 42 D10
Hillsdale 42 E3
Hillston 32 B4
Hilton Head Island 43 J5
Hilversum 16 B2
Himachal Pradesh □ 25 B6
Himalaya 25 C7
Himeji 22 F4
Ḥimş 24 B2
Hinckley, *U.K.* 9 E6
Hinckley, *U.S.A.* 40 B8
Hindmarsh, L. 32 C3
Hindu Kush 25 B6
Hinesville 43 K5
Hingham 38 B8
Hinton 42 G5
Hios 15 E12
Hirosaki 22 C7
Hiroshima 22 F3
Hispaniola 45 D10
Hitachi 22 E7
Hitchin 9 F7
Hiva Oa 35 H14
Hjälmaren 7 F7
Hoa Binh 23 A2
Hoare B. 37 C13
Hobart, *Australia* 32 D4
Hobart, *U.S.A.* 41 H5
Hobbs 41 J3
Hobe Sound 43 M5
Hodgson 36 D10
Hōfu 22 F2
Hogan Group 32 C4
Hohenwald 43 H2
Hohhot 21 B6
Hoisington 40 F5
Hokianga Harbour 33 F4
Hokitika 33 K3
Hokkaidō □ 22 B8
Holbrook, *Australia* 32 C4
Holbrook, *U.S.A.* 39 J8
Holden 38 G7
Holdenville 41 H6
Holdrege 40 E5
Holetown 45 g
Holguín 45 C9
Holland 42 D2
Hollandale 41 J9
Hollidaysburg 42 E6
Hollis 41 H5
Hollister, *Calif.*, *U.S.A.* 39 H3
Hollister, *Idaho*, *U.S.A.* 38 E6
Holly Hill 43 L5
Holly Springs 41 H10
Hollywood 43 N5
Holman 36 B8
Holmen 40 D9
Holsworthy 9 G3
Holton 40 F7
Holtville 39 K6
Holy I., *Anglesey*, *U.K.* 8 D3
Holy I., *Northumberland*, *U.K.* 8 B6
Holyhead 8 D3
Holyoke, *Colo.*, *U.S.A.* 40 E3
Holyoke, *Mass.*, *U.S.A.* 42 D9
Home B. 37 C13
Homedale 38 E5
Homer, *Alaska*, *U.S.A.* 36 D4
Homer, *La.*, *U.S.A.* 41 J8
Homestead 43 N5
Homestead △ 40 E6
Homs = Ḥimş 24 B2
Homyel 18 D4
Hondo 41 L5
Honduras ■ 44 E7
Honduras, G. de 44 D7
Honey L. 38 F3
Hong → 20 D5
Hong Gai 23 A2
Hong Kong □ 21 G11
Hong Kong I. 21 G11
Hong Kong Int. (HKG) 21 G10
Hongjiang 21 D5
Hongshui He → 21 D5
Hongze Hu 21 C6
Honiara 31 B10
Honiton 9 G4
Honolulu 35 E12
Honshū 22 F6
Hood, Mt. 38 D3
Hood River 38 D3
Hoodsport 38 C2
Hook Hd. 11 D5
Hooker 41 G4
Hooper Bay 36 C3
Hoopeston 42 E2
Hoorn 16 B2
Hoover 43 J2
Hoover Dam 39 J6
Hope 41 J8
Hope, L. 32 A2
Hopedale 37 D13
Hopetoun 32 C3
Hopewell 42 G7
Hopkinsville 43 G2
Hopland 38 G2
Hoquiam 38 C2
Horlivka 17 A5
Hormuz, Str. of 24 C4
Horn, Cape = Hornos, C. de 48 H3
Horn, Is. 31 C15
Horn Head 11 A3
Hornavan 7 D7
Hornbeck 41 K8
Hornbrook 38 F2
Horncastle 8 D7
Hornell 42 D7
Hornos, C. de 48 H3
Hornsea 8 D7
Horqin Youyi Qianqi 21 B7
Horse Cr. → 40 E3
Horsham, *Australia* 32 C3
Horsham, *U.K.* 9 F7
Horton 40 F7
Horton → 36 C7
Hot Creek Range 38 G6
Hot Springs, *Ark.*, *U.S.A.* 41 H8
Hot Springs, *S. Dak.*, *U.S.A.* 40 D3
Hot Springs △ 41 H8
Hotan 20 C2
Hotchkiss 39 G10
Hou Hai 21 F10
Houghton 40 B10
Houghton L. 42 C3
Houghton-le-Spring 8 C6
Houhora Heads 33 F4
Houlton 43 B12
Houma 41 L9
Houston, *Mo.*, *U.S.A.* 41 G9
Houston, *Tex.*, *U.S.A.* 41 L7
Hovd □ 20 B4
Hove 9 G7
Hovenweep △ 39 H9
Hövsgöl Nuur 20 A5
Howard, *Australia* 32 A5
Howard, *U.S.A.* 40 C6
Howe 38 E7
Howe, C. 32 C5
Howell 42 D4
Howitt, L. 32 A2
Howland I. 34 G10
Howrah = Haora 25 C7
Howth 11 C5
Howth Hd. 11 C5
Hoy 10 C5
Høyanger 7 E5
Hoylake 8 D4
Hradec Králové 16 C7
Hrodna 18 D3
Hron → 16 E9
Hsinchu 21 D7
Hua Hin 23 B1
Huahine, Î. 35 J12
Huai He → 21 C6
Huainan 21 C6
Huaiyin 21 C6
Hualapai Peak 39 J7
Huambo 29 G3
Huancayo 46 F3
Huang He → 21 C6
Huangshan 21 D6
Huangshi 21 C6
Huánuco 46 E3
Huascarán, Nevado 46 E3
Huatabampo 44 B3
Hubbard 41 K6
Hubei □ 21 C6
Hubli 25 D6
Hucknall 8 D6
Huddersfield 8 D6
Hudiksvall 7 E7
Hudson, *N.Y.*, *U.S.A.* 42 D9
Hudson, *Wis.*, *U.S.A.* 40 C8
Hudson, *Wyo.*, *U.S.A.* 38 E9
Hudson → 42 E8
Hudson Bay 37 D11
Hudson Falls 42 D9
Hudson Str. 37 C13
Hue 23 B2
Huelva 13 D2
Huesca 13 A5
Hughenden 30 E7
Hugo, *Colo.*, *U.S.A.* 40 F3
Hugo, *Okla.*, *U.S.A.* 41 H7
Hugoton 41 G4
Huize 20 D5
Hull 37 E12
Hull → 8 D7
Hulun Nur 21 B6
Humacao 45 d
Humber → 8 D7
Humboldt, *Canada* 36 D9
Humboldt, *Iowa*, *U.S.A.* 40 D7
Humboldt, *Tenn.*, *U.S.A.* 41 H10
Humboldt → 38 F4
Hume, L. 32 C4
Humen 21 F10
Humphreys Peak 39 J8
Hunan □ 21 D6
Hungary ■ 16 E9
Hungerford 32 A3
Hŭngnam 21 C7
Hunsrück 16 D3
Hunstanton 8 E8
Hunter I. 32 D3
Hunter Ra. 32 B5
Hunterville 33 H5
Huntingburg 42 F2
Huntingdon, *U.K.* 9 E7
Huntingdon, *U.S.A.* 42 E7
Huntington, *Ind.*, *U.S.A.* 42 E3
Huntington, *Oreg.*, *U.S.A.* 38 D5
Huntington, *Utah*, *U.S.A.* 38 G8
Huntington, *W. Va.*, *U.S.A.* 42 F4
Huntington Beach 39 K5
Huntly, *N.Z.* 33 G5
Huntly, *U.K.* 10 D6
Huntsville, *Canada* 37 E12
Huntsville, *Ala.*, *U.S.A.* 43 H2
Huntsville, *Tex.*, *U.S.A.* 41 K7
Huonville 32 D4
Hurghada 24 C2
Hurley, *N. Mex.*, *U.S.A.* 39 K9
Hurley, *Wis.*, *U.S.A.* 40 B9
Huron 40 C5
Huron, L. 42 C4
Hurricane 39 H7
Hurunui → 33 K4
Hutchinson, *Kans.*, *U.S.A.* 41 F6
Hutchinson, *Minn.*, *U.S.A.* 40 C7
Hutton, Mt. 32 A4
Huzhou 21 C7
Hwang Ho = Huang He → 21 C6
Hyannis, *Mass.*, *U.S.A.* 42 E10
Hyannis, *Nebr.*, *U.S.A.* 40 E4
Hyargas Nuur 20 B4
Hyderabad, *India* 25 D6
Hyderabad, *Pakistan* 24 C5
Hyères 12 E7
Hyères, Îs. d' 12 E7
Hyndman Peak 38 E6
Hyrum 38 F8
Hysham 38 C10
Hythe 9 F9

I

Ialomiţa → 15 B12
Iaşi 17 A3
Ibadan 26 G6
Ibagué 46 C3
Ibb 24 D3
Iberian Peninsula 2 B9
Ibiza = Eivissa 13 C6
'Ibrī 24 C4
Ica 46 F3
İçel 17 C4
Iceland ■ 7 B2
Ichihara 22 F7
Ichinomiya 22 F5
Ida Grove 40 D7
Idabel 41 J7
Idaho □ 38 D7
Idaho City 38 E6
Idaho Falls 38 E7
Idar-Oberstein 16 D3
Ife 26 G6
Igarka 18 C9
Iglésias 14 E3
Igloolik 37 C11
Iguaçu, Cat. del 48 B6
Iguala 44 D5
Iisalmi 7 E9
IJsselmeer 16 B2
Ikaluktutiak 36 C9
Ikeda 22 F3
Ilagan 23 B4
Ile → 18 E8
Île-de-France □ 12 B5
Ilesha 26 G6
Ilfracombe 9 F3
Ilhéus 47 F11
Iliamna L. 36 D4
Iligan 23 C4
Ilkeston 8 E6
Ilkley 8 D6
Iller → 16 D4
Illinois □ 40 E10
Illinois → 40 F9
Iloilo 23 B4
Ilorin 26 G6
Imabari 22 F3
Imbil 32 A5
imeni Ismail Samani, Pik 18 F8
Imi 24 E3
Imlay 38 F4
Immingham 8 D7
Immokalee 43 M5
Imperatriz 47 E9
Imperial 40 E4
Imperial Dam 39 K6
Imphal 25 C8
Inangahua 33 J3
Inari 7 D9
Inarijärvi 7 D9
Incheon 21 C7
Incline Village 38 G4
Incomáti → 29 K6
Indalsälven → 7 E7
Independence, *Calif.*, *U.S.A.* 39 H4
Independence, *Iowa*, *U.S.A.* 40 D9
Independence, *Kans.*, *U.S.A.* 41 G7
Independence, *Ky.*, *U.S.A.* 42 F3
Independence, *Mo.*, *U.S.A.* 40 F7
Independence Mts. 38 F5
India ■ 25 C6
Indian → 43 M5
Indian Ocean 3 E14
Indian Springs 39 G6
Indiana 42 E6
Indiana □ 42 F3
Indianapolis 42 F2
Indianola, *Iowa*, *U.S.A.* 40 E8
Indianola, *Miss.*, *U.S.A.* 41 J9
Indigirka → 19 B15
Indio 39 K5
Indo-China 23 B2
Indonesia ■ 23 D3
Indore 25 C6
Indravati → 25 D7
Indre → 12 C4
Indulkana 32 A1
Indus → 24 C5
Indus, Mouths of the 24 C5
Ingleborough 8 C5
Inglewood, *Queens.*, *Australia* 32 A5
Inglewood, *Vic.*, *Australia* 32 C3
Inglewood, *N.Z.* 33 H5
Inglewood, *U.S.A.* 39 K4
Ingolstadt 16 D5
Ingomar 38 C10
Inishbofin 11 C1
Inisheer 11 C2
Inishfree B. 11 A3
Inishkea North 11 B1
Inishkea South 11 B1
Inishmaan 11 C2
Inishmore 11 C2
Inishmurray I. 11 B3
Inishowen Pen. 11 A4
Inishshark 11 C1
Inishturk 11 C1
Inishvickillane 11 D1
Injune 32 A4
Inland Kaikoura Ra. 33 J4
Inn → 16 D6
Innamincka 32 A3
Inner Hebrides 10 E2
Inner Mongolia = Nei Monggol Zizhiqu □ 21 B6
Inner Sound 10 D3
Innsbruck 16 E5
Inny → 11 C4
Inowrocław 16 B9
Insein 25 D8
Interlaken 12 C7
International Falls 40 A8
Inukjuak 37 D12
Inuvik 36 C6
Inveraray 10 E3
Inverbervie 10 E6
Invercargill 33 M2
Inverclyde □ 10 F4
Inverell 32 A5
Invergordon 10 D4
Inverloch 32 C4
Inverness, *U.K.* 10 D4
Inverness, *U.S.A.* 43 L4
Inverurie 10 D6
Investigator Group 32 B1
Investigator Str. 32 C2
Inyo Mts. 39 H5
Inyokern 39 J5
Iola 41 G7
Iona 10 E2
Ione 38 G3
Ionia 42 D3
Ionian Is. = Ionioi Nisoi 15 E9
Ionian Sea 15 E7
Ionioi Nisoi 15 E9
Iowa □ 40 D8
Iowa → 40 E9
Iowa City 40 E9
Iowa Falls 40 D8
Iowa Park 41 J5
Ipatinga 47 G10
Ipoh 23 C2
Ipswich, *Australia* 32 A5
Ipswich, *U.K.* 9 E9
Ipswich, *U.S.A.* 40 C5
Iqaluit 37 C13
Iquique 46 H4
Iquitos 46 D4
Iraklio 15 G11
Iran ■ 24 B4
Irapuato 44 C4
Iraq ■ 24 B3
Ireland ■ 11 C4
Iringa 28 F7
Irish Republic ■ 11 C4
Irish Sea 8 D3
Irkutsk 19 D11
Iron Baron 32 B2
Iron Knob 32 B2
Iron Mountain 42 C1
Iron River 40 B10
Ironton, *Mo.*, *U.S.A.* 41 G9
Ironton, *Ohio*, *U.S.A.* 42 F4
Ironwood 40 B9
Ironwood Forest △ 39 K8
Irrara Cr. → 32 A4
Irrawaddy → 25 D8
Irtysh → 18 C7
Irvine, *U.K.* 10 F4
Irvine, *U.S.A.* 42 G4
Irvinestown 11 B4
Irving 41 J6
Irymple 32 B3
Isabel 40 C4
Isabela 45 d
Isar → 16 D6
Isère → 12 D6
Isfahan = Eşfahān 24 B4
Ishim → 18 D8
Ishinomaki 22 D7
Ishpeming 42 B2
İskenderun 17 C5
Isla → 10 E5
Islamabad 25 B6
Island L. 36 D10
Island Lagoon 32 B2
Island Pond 42 C10
Islands, B. of 33 F5
Islay 10 F2
Isle of Wight □ 9 G6
Isle Royale △ 42 B1
Ismâ'ilîya 27 B12
Israel ■ 17 D4
Issoire 12 D5
İstanbul 15 D13
İstanbul Boğazı 15 D13
Istokpoga, L. 43 M5
Istra 14 B6
Istres 12 E6
Istria = Istra 14 B6
Itabuna 47 F11
Itaipú, Represa de 48 B6
Italy ■ 14 C5
Itapipoca 47 D11
Itchen → 9 G6
Ithaca 42 D7
Ivanhoe, *Australia* 32 B3
Ivanhoe, *U.S.A.* 40 C6
Ivano-Frankivsk 18 E3
Ivanovo 18 D5
Ivory Coast ■ 26 G4
Ivujivik 37 C12
Ivybridge 9 G4
Iwaki 22 E7
Iwakuni 22 F3
Iwo 26 G6
Izhevsk 18 D6
Izkī 24 C4
İzmir 15 E12

J

J. Strom Thurmond L. 43 J4
Jabalpur 25 C6
Jaboatão 47 E11
Jackman 43 C10
Jacksboro 41 J5
Jackson, *Barbados* 45 g
Jackson, *Ala.*, *U.S.A.* 43 K2
Jackson, *Calif.*, *U.S.A.* 38 G3
Jackson, *Ky.*, *U.S.A.* 42 G4
Jackson, *Mich.*, *U.S.A.* 42 D3
Jackson, *Minn.*, *U.S.A.* 40 D7
Jackson, *Miss.*, *U.S.A.* 41 J9
Jackson, *Mo.*, *U.S.A.* 41 G10
Jackson, *Ohio*, *U.S.A.* 42 F4
Jackson, *Tenn.*, *U.S.A.* 43 H1
Jackson, *Wyo.*, *U.S.A.* 38 E8
Jackson B. 33 K2
Jackson L. 38 E8
Jacksons 33 K3
Jacksonville, *Ala.*, *U.S.A.* 43 J3
Jacksonville, *Ark.*, *U.S.A.* 41 H8
Jacksonville, *Fla.*, *U.S.A.* 43 K5
Jacksonville, *Ill.*, *U.S.A.* 40 F9
Jacksonville, *N.C.*, *U.S.A.* 43 H7
Jacksonville, *Tex.*, *U.S.A.* 41 K7
Jacksonville Beach 43 K5
Jacmel 45 D10
Jacob Lake 39 H7
Jaén 13 D4
Jaffa = Tel Aviv-Yafo 17 D4
Jaffa, C. 32 C2
Jaffna 25 E7
Jagdalpur 25 D7
Jahrom 24 C4
Jaipur 25 C6
Jakarta 23 D2
Jal 41 J3
Jalna 25 D6
Jaluit I. 34 G8
Jamaica ■ 44 a
Jambi 23 D2
James →, *S. Dak.*, *U.S.A.* 40 D6
James →, *Va.*, *U.S.A.* 42 G7
James B. 37 D12
Jamestown, *Australia* 32 B2
Jamestown, *N. Dak.*, *U.S.A.* 40 B5
Jamestown, *N.Y.*, *U.S.A.* 42 D6
Jammu 25 B6
Jammu & Kashmir □ 25 B6
Jamnagar 25 C6
Jamshedpur 25 C7
Jan Mayen 6 B6
Jandowae 32 A5
Janesville 40 D10
Japan ■ 22 F5
Japan, Sea of 22 D4
Japan Trench 34 D6
Japurá → 46 D5
Jarvis I. 35 H12
Jāsk 24 C4
Jasper, *Canada* 36 D8
Jasper, *Ala.*, *U.S.A.* 43 J2
Jasper, *Fla.*, *U.S.A.* 43 K4
Jasper, *Ind.*, *U.S.A.* 42 F2
Jasper, *Tex.*, *U.S.A.* 41 K8
Jaunpur 25 C7
Java = Jawa 23 D3
Java Sea 23 D2
Java Trench 23 D2
Jawa 23 D3
Jaya, Puncak 23 D5
Jayton 41 J4
Jean 39 J6
Jeanerette 41 L9
Jebel, Bahr el → 27 G12
Jedburgh 10 F6
Jedda = Jiddah 24 C2
Jefferson, *Iowa*, *U.S.A.* 40 D7
Jefferson, *Tex.*, *U.S.A.* 41 J7
Jefferson, Mt., *Nev.*, *U.S.A.* 38 G5
Jefferson, Mt., *Oreg.*, *U.S.A.* 38 D3
Jefferson City, *Mo.*, *U.S.A.* 40 F8
Jefferson City, *Tenn.*, *U.S.A.* 43 G4
Jeffersontown 42 F3
Jeffersonville 42 F3
Jeffrey City 38 E10
Jeju-do 21 C7
Jekyll I. 43 K5
Jelenia Góra 16 C7
Jena, *Germany* 16 C5
Jena, *U.S.A.* 41 K8
Jenkins 42 G4
Jennings 41 K8
Jeonju 21 C7
Jeparit 32 C3
Jequié 47 F10
Jérémie 45 D10
Jerez de la Frontera 13 D2
Jerilderie 32 C4
Jerome 38 E6
Jersey 9 H5
Jersey City 42 E8
Jersey Shore 42 E7
Jerseyville 40 F9
Jerusalem 17 D5
Jervis B. 32 C5
Jesup 43 K5
Jetmore 41 F5
Jhansi 25 C6
Jharkhand □ 25 C7
Jhelum → 25 B6

Manihiki Plateau

Jiamusi 21 B8
Ji'an 21 D6
Jiangcheng 20 D5
Jiangmen 21 D6
Jiangsu □ 21 C7
Jiangxi □ 21 D6
Jiaxing 21 C7
Jiddah 24 C2
Jihlava → 16 D8
Jijiga 24 E3
Jilin 21 B7
Jilin □ 21 B7
Jiménez 44 B4
Jinan 21 C6
Jinchang 20 C5
Jindabyne 32 C4
Jinding 21 G10
Jingdezhen 21 D6
Jinggu 20 D5
Jinhua 21 D6
Jining, Nei Monggol Zizhiqu, China 21 B6
Jining, Shandong, China 21 C6
Jinja 28 D6
Jinsha Jiang → 20 D5
Jinzhou 21 B7
Jiujiang 21 D6
Jiwani 24 C5
Jixi 21 B8
Jīzān 24 D3
Jizzakh 24 A5
João Pessoa 47 E12
Jodhpur 25 C6
Johannesburg 29 K5
John Crow Mts. 44 a
John Day 38 D4
John Day → 38 D3
John Day Fossil Beds △ 38 D4
John H. Kerr Res. 43 G6
John o' Groats 10 C5
Johnson City, Kans., U.S.A. 41 G4
Johnson City, Tenn., U.S.A. 43 G4
Johnson City, Tex., U.S.A. 41 K5
Johnston I. 35 F11
Johnstown, Ireland 11 D4
Johnstown, N.Y., U.S.A. 42 D8
Johnstown, Pa., U.S.A. 42 E6
Johor Bahru 23 C2
Joinville 48 B7
Joliet 42 E1
Joliette 37 E12
Jolo 23 C4
Jones Sound 37 B10
Jonesboro, Ark., U.S.A. 41 H9
Jonesboro, La., U.S.A. 41 J8
Jönköping 7 F6
Jonquière 37 E12
Joplin 41 G7
Jordan 38 C10
Jordan ■ 24 B2
Jordan → 17 D5
Jordan Valley 38 E5
Jos 26 G7
Joseph Bonaparte G. 30 C4
Joshua Tree △ 39 K5
Jost Van Dyke I. 45 e
Jotunheimen 7 E5
Jourdanton 41 L5
Juan de Fuca, Str of. 38 B1
Juan Fernández, Arch. de 35 L20
Juàzeiro do Norte 47 E11
Juchitán de Zaragoza 44 D5
Judith → 38 C9
Judith Gap 38 C9
Juiz de Fora 47 H10
Julesburg 40 E3
Juliaca 46 G4
Jullundur 25 B6
Junagadh 25 C6
Junction, Tex., U.S.A. 41 K5
Junction, Utah, U.S.A. 39 G7
Junction City, Kans., U.S.A. 40 F6
Junction City, Oreg., U.S.A. 38 D2
Jundiaí 48 A7
Juneau 36 D6
Junee 32 B4
Junggar Pendi 20 B3
Juntura 38 E4
Jura 10 F3
Jura, Mts. du 12 C7
Jura, Sd. of 10 F3
Juruá → 46 D5
Jutland = Jylland 7 F5
Juventud, I. de la 45 C8
Jylland 7 F5
Jyväskylä 7 E9

K

K2 25 B6
Kabaena 23 D4
Kābul 25 B5
Kabwe 29 G5
Kachchh, Gulf of 25 C5
Kachin □ 25 C8
Kadavu 33 D8
Kadina 32 B2
Kadoka 40 D4
Kaduna 26 F7
Kaesŏng 21 C7
Kagoshima 22 H2
Kahoka 40 E9
Kahramanmaraş 17 C5
Kahurangi △ 33 J4
Kai, Kepulauan 23 D5
Kaiapoi 33 K4
Kaifeng 21 C6
Kaikohe 33 F4
Kaikoura 33 K4
Kaimanawa Mts. 33 H5
Kaipara Harbour 33 G5
Kaiserslautern 16 D3
Kaitaia 33 F4
Kaitangata 33 M2
Kajaani 7 E9
Kajabbi 30 D7
Kakanui Mts. 33 L3
Kakinada 25 D7
Kalaallit Nunaat = Greenland ☒ 6 C4
Kalahari 29 J4
Kalama 38 D2
Kalamazoo 42 D3
Kalamazoo → 42 D2
Kalemie 28 F5
Kalgoorlie-Boulder 30 G3
Kalimantan 23 D3
Kaliningrad 16 A10
Kalispell 38 B6
Kalisz 16 C9
Kalkaska 42 C3
Kalmar 7 F7
Kaluga 18 D4
Kamchatka, Poluostrov 19 D16
Kamensk Uralskiy 18 D7
Kamiah 38 C5
Kamina 28 F5
Kamloops 36 D7
Kampala 28 D6
Kampong Saom 23 B2
Kamyanets-Podilskyy 17 A3
Kamyshin 18 D5
Kanaaupscow 37 D12
Kanab 39 H7
Kanab Cr. → 39 H7
Kananga 28 F4
Kanawha → 42 F4
Kanazawa 22 E5
Kandanghaur 23 D2
Kandos 32 B4
Kandy 25 E7
Kane 42 E6
Kane Basin 6 B3
Kangaroo I. 32 C2
Kangean, Kepulauan 23 D3
Kangiqsualujjuaq 37 D13
Kangiqsujuaq 37 C12
Kangirsuk 37 D13
Kanin, Poluostrov 18 C5
Kaniva 32 C3
Kankakee 42 E2
Kankakee → 42 E1
Kankan 26 F4
Kannapolis 43 H5
Kano 26 F7
Kanpur 25 C7
Kansas □ 40 F6
Kansas → 40 F7
Kansas City, Kans., U.S.A. 40 F7
Kansas City, Mo., U.S.A. 40 F7
Kansk 19 D10
Kanturk 11 D3
Kanye 29 J5
Kaohsiung 21 D7
Kaolack 26 F2
Kapiti I. 33 J5
Kaplan 41 K8
Kaposvár 16 E8
Kapuas → 23 D2
Kapuas Hulu, Pegunungan 23 C3
Kapunda 32 B2
Kapuni 33 H5
Kaputar, Mt. 32 B5
Kara Kum = Garagum 18 F6
Kara Sea 18 B7
Karachi 24 C5
Karaganda = Qaraghandy 18 E8
Karaj 24 B4
Karakol 25 A6
Karakoram Ra. 25 B6
Karamay 20 B3
Karamea Bight 33 J3
Karasburg 29 K3
Karawang 23 D2
Karbalā' 24 B3
Karimata, Kepulauan 23 D2
Karimata, Selat 23 D2
Karimunjawa, Kepulauan 23 D3
Karlskrona 7 F7
Karlsruhe 16 D4
Karlstad, Sweden 7 F6
Karlstad, U.S.A. 40 A6
Karnataka □ 25 D6
Karnes City 41 L6
Karnische Alpen 14 A5
Kärnten □ 16 E6
Karoonda 32 C2
Karora 24 D2
Karratha 30 E2
Karsakpay 18 E7
Karufa 23 D5
Kasai → 28 E3
Kasba L. 36 C9
Kāshān 24 B4
Kashi 20 C2
Kaskaskia → 40 G10
Kassalâ 27 E13
Kassel 16 C4
Kasson 40 C8
Katahdin, Mt. 43 C11
Katanga □ 28 F4
Katha 25 C8
Katherine 30 C5
Katmandu 25 C7
Katoomba 32 B5
Katowice 16 C9
Katrine, L. 10 E4
Katsina 26 F7
Kattegat 7 F6
Kaufman 41 J6
Kaukauna 42 C1
Kaunas 18 D3
Kavala 15 D11
Kavieng 30 A9
Kavīr, Dasht-e 24 B4
Kawagoe 22 F6
Kawaguchi 22 F6
Kawasaki 22 F6
Kawawachikamach 37 D13
Kawerau 33 H6
Kawhia 33 H5
Kawhia Harbour 33 H5
Kayan → 23 C3
Kaycee 38 E10
Kayenta 39 H8
Kayes 26 F3
Kayseri 17 C5
Kaysville 38 F8
Kazakhstan ■ 18 E7
Kazan 18 D5
Kazan-Rettō 34 E6
Kāzerūn 24 C4
Keady 11 B5
Kearney 40 E5
Kearny 39 K8
Kebnekaise 7 D7
Kebri Dehar 24 E3
Kebumen 23 D2
Kecskemét 16 E9
Kediri 23 D3
Keeling Is. = Cocos Is. 23 E1
Keene 42 D9
Keeper Hill 11 D3
Keetmanshoop 29 K3
Kefalonia 15 E9
Keighley 8 D6
Keith, Australia 32 C3
Keith, U.K. 10 D6
Keizer 38 D2
Kellogg 38 C5
Kelowna 36 E8
Kelso, N.Z. 33 L2
Kelso, U.K. 10 F6
Kelso, U.S.A. 38 C2
Kemerovo 18 D9
Kemi 7 D8
Kemijoki → 7 D8
Kemmerer 38 F8
Kemp, L. 41 J5
Kemp Land 6 D9
Kempsey 32 B5
Kempton 32 D4
Kenai 36 C4
Kendal 8 C5
Kendall, Australia 32 B5
Kendall, U.S.A. 43 N5
Kendallville 42 E3
Kendari 23 D4
Kenedy 41 L6
Kenhardt 29 K4
Kenitra 26 B4
Kenmare, Ireland 11 E2
Kenmare, U.S.A. 40 A3
Kenmare River 11 E2
Kennebec 40 D5
Kennebec → 43 D11
Kenner 41 L9
Kennet → 9 F7
Kennett 41 G9
Kennewick 38 C4
Kenogami → 37 D11
Kenora 36 E10
Kenosha 42 D2
Kent, Tex., U.S.A. 41 K2
Kent, Wash., U.S.A. 38 C2
Kent □ 9 F8
Kent Group 32 C4
Kent Pen. 36 C9
Kentland 42 E2
Kenton 42 E4
Kentucky □ 42 G3
Kentucky → 42 F3
Kentucky L. 43 G2
Kentville 37 E13
Kentwood 41 K9
Kenya ■ 28 D7
Kenya, Mt. 28 E7
Keokuk 40 E9
Kerala □ 25 D6
Kerang 32 C3
Kerch 17 A5
Kerguelen 5 G14
Kerinci 23 D2
Kerkyra 15 E8
Kermadec Is. 31 G15
Kermadec Trench 31 G15
Kermān 24 B4
Kermānshāh 24 B3
Kermit 41 K3
Kern → 39 J4
Kerrera 10 E3
Kerrobert 36 D9
Kerrville 41 K5
Kerry □ 11 D2
Kerry Hd. 11 D2
Kerulen → 21 B6
Keswick 8 C4
Ketchikan 36 D6
Ketchum 38 E6
Kettering, U.K. 9 E7
Kettering, U.S.A. 42 F3
Kettle Falls 38 B4
Kewanee 40 E10
Kewaunee 42 C2
Keweenaw B. 42 B1
Keweenaw Pen. 42 B2
Keweenaw Pt. 42 B2
Key, L. 11 C3
Key Largo 43 N5
Keynsham 9 F5
Keyser 42 F6
Khabarovsk 19 E14
Khambhat, G. of 25 C6
Khamīs Mushayţ 24 D3
Kharagpur 25 C7
Kharkiv 18 E4
Kharkov = Kharkiv 18 E4
Khartoum = El Khartûm 27 E12
Khaskovo 15 D11
Khatanga 19 B11
Kherson 17 A4
Kholm 24 B5
Khon Kaen 23 B2
Khorramābād 24 B4
Khorrāmshahr 24 B3
Khorugh 25 B6
Khouribga 26 B4
Khŭjand 18 E7
Khulna 25 C7
Khvoy 24 B3
Khyber Pass 25 B6
Kiama 32 B5
Kicking Horse Pass 36 D8
Kidderminster 9 E5
Kidnappers, C. 33 H6
Kidsgrove 8 D5
Kiel 16 A5
Kiel Canal = Nord-Ostsee-Kanal 16 A4
Kielce 16 C10
Kielder Water 8 B5
Kiev = Kyyiv 18 D4
Kigali 28 E6
Kigoma-Ujiji 28 E5
Kikwit 28 E3
Kilbeggan 11 C4
Kilbrannan Sd. 10 F3
Kilcoy 32 A5
Kildare 11 C5
Kildare □ 11 C5
Kilfinnane 11 D3
Kilgarvan 11 E2
Kilgore 41 J7
Kilimanjaro 28 E7
Kilkee 11 D2
Kilkeel 11 B5
Kilkenny 11 D4
Kilkenny □ 11 D4
Kilkieran B. 11 C2
Killala 11 B2
Killala B. 11 B2
Killaloe 11 D3
Killarney, Australia 32 A5
Killarney, Ireland 11 D2
Killarney △ 11 D2
Killary Harbour 11 C2
Killdeer 40 B3
Killeen 41 K6
Killin 10 E4
Killiney 11 C5
Killorglin 11 D2
Killybegs 11 B3
Kilmarnock 10 F4
Kilmore 32 C3
Kilmore Quay 11 D5
Kilrush 11 D2
Kilwinning 10 F4
Kim 41 G3
Kimba 32 B2
Kimball, Nebr., U.S.A. 40 E3
Kimball, S. Dak., U.S.A. 40 D5
Kimberley, Australia 30 D4
Kimberley, S. Africa 29 K4
Kimberly 38 E6
Kimmirut 37 C13
Kinabalu, Gunung 23 C3
Kinder Scout 8 D6
Kindersley 36 D9
Kindu 28 E5
King City 39 H3
King George I. 6 D4
King George Is. 37 D11
King I. 32 C3
King William I. 36 C10
Kingaroy 32 A5
Kingfisher 41 H6
Kingman, Ariz., U.S.A. 39 J6
Kingman, Kans., U.S.A. 41 G5
Kingoonya 32 B2
Kings → 39 H4
Kings Canyon △ 39 H4
King's Lynn 8 E8
Kings Peak 38 F8
Kingsbridge 9 G4
Kingsburg 39 H4
Kingscote 32 C2
Kingscourt 11 C5
Kingsford 42 C1
Kingsland 43 K5
Kingsport 43 G4
Kingston, Canada 37 E12
Kingston, Jamaica 44 a
Kingston, N.Z. 33 L2
Kingston, N.Y., U.S.A. 42 E9
Kingston, Pa., U.S.A. 42 E8
Kingston South East 32 C2
Kingston upon Hull 8 D7
Kingston-upon-Thames □ 9 F7
Kingstown 45 E12
Kingstree 43 J6
Kingsville 41 M6
Kingussie 10 D4
Kingwood 41 K7
Kinleith 33 H5
Kinlochleven 10 E4
Kinnairds Hd. 10 D6
Kinross 10 E5
Kinsale 11 E3
Kinsale, Old Hd. of 11 E3
Kinshasa 28 E3
Kinsley 41 G5
Kinston 43 H7
Kintore 10 D6
Kintyre 10 F3
Kintyre, Mull of 10 F3
Kinvarra 11 C3
Kiowa, Kans., U.S.A. 41 G5
Kiowa, Okla., U.S.A. 41 H7
Kippure 11 C5
Kirensk 19 D11
Kirghizia = Kyrgyzstan ■ 18 E8
Kiribati ■ 31 A15
Kırıkkale 17 C4
Kiritimati 35 G12
Kirkby 8 D5
Kirkby-in-Ashfield 8 D6
Kirkby Lonsdale 8 C5
Kirkby Stephen 8 C5
Kirkcaldy 10 E5
Kirkcudbright 10 G4
Kirkintilloch 10 F4
Kirkland Lake 37 E11
Kirksville 40 E8
Kirkūk 24 B3
Kirkwall 10 C6
Kirov 18 D5
Kirovohrad 17 A4
Kirriemuir 10 E5
Kirtland 39 H9
Kiruna 7 D8
Kiryū 22 E6
Kisangani 28 D5
Kishinev = Chişinău 17 A3
Kislovodsk 17 B6
Kissimmee 43 L5
Kissimmee → 43 M5
Kisumu 28 E6
Kit Carson 40 F3
Kitakyūshū 22 G2
Kitami 22 B8
Kitchener 37 E11
Kitimat 36 D7
Kittakittaooloo, L. 32 A2
Kittanning 42 E6
Kittery 43 D10
Kitwe 29 G5
Kivu, L. 28 E5
Kızıl Irmak → 17 B5
Kladno 16 C7
Klagenfurt 16 E7
Klaipėda 18 D3
Klamath → 38 F1
Klamath Falls 38 E3
Klamath Mts. 38 F2
Klang 23 C2
Klarälven → 7 F6
Klerksdorp 29 K5
Klickitat 38 D3
Kluane L. 36 C6
Kluang 23 C2
Klyuchevskaya, Gora 19 D17
Knaresborough 8 C6
Knighton 9 E4
Knock 11 C3
Knockmealdown Mts. 11 D4
Knossos 15 G11
Knox 42 E2
Knoxville, Iowa, U.S.A. 40 E8
Knoxville, Tenn., U.S.A. 43 H4
Kōbe 22 F4
København 7 F6
Koblenz 16 C3
Kocaeli 17 B3
Kōchi 22 G3
Kodiak 36 D4
Kodiak I. 36 D4
Koforidua 26 G5
Kōfu 22 F6
Kokkola 7 E8
Kokomo 42 E2
Kökshetaū 18 D7
Koksoak → 37 D13
Kokstad 29 L5
Kolaka 23 D4
Kolar 25 D6
Kolhapur 25 D6
Kolkata 25 C7
Köln 16 C3
Kolomna 18 D4
Kolskiy Poluostrov 7 D11
Kolwezi 28 G5
Kolyma → 19 C17
Kolymskoye Nagorye 19 C16
Komandorskiye Ostrova 19 D17
Komatsu 22 E5
Kompong Cham 23 B2
Komsomolets, Ostrov 19 A10
Komsomolsk 19 D14
Konin 16 B9
Konya 17 C4
Koocanusa, L. 38 B6
Koonibba 32 B1
Koorawatha 32 B4
Kooskia 38 C6
Kootenay L. 38 B5
Kopet Dagh 24 B4
Kopi 32 B2
Korçë 15 D9
Korea, North ■ 21 C7
Korea, South ■ 21 C7
Korea Bay 21 C7
Korea Strait 21 C7
Korinthiakos Kolpos 15 E10
Kōriyama 22 E7
Korla 20 B3
Koro 33 C8
Koro Sea 33 C9
Koror 34 G5
Körös → 16 E10
Kortrijk 16 C1
Kos 15 F12
Kosciusko 41 J10
Kosciuszko, Mt. 32 C4
Kosovo □ 15 C9
Kôstî 27 F12
Kostroma 18 D5
Koszalin 16 A8
Kota 25 C6
Kota Bharu 23 C2
Kota Kinabalu 23 C3
Kotabumi 23 D2
Kotka 7 E9
Kotuy → 19 B11
Kotzebue 36 C3
Kounradskiy 18 E8
Kountze 41 K7
Kowloon 21 G11
Kozhikode = Calicut 25 D6
Kra, Isthmus of = Kra, Kho Khot 23 B1
Kra, Kho Khot 23 B1
Kragujevac 15 B9
Krakatau = Rakata, Pulau 23 D2
Kraków 16 C9
Kramatorsk 17 A5
Krasnodar 17 A5
Krasnoyarsk 19 D10
Krasnyy Luch 17 A5
Krefeld 16 C3
Kremenchuk 17 A4
Kremmling 38 F10
Krishna → 25 D7
Kristiansand 7 F5
Kristiansund 7 E5
Kriti 15 G11
Kroonstad 29 K5
Krugersdorp 29 K5
Krung Thep = Bangkok 23 B2
Kruševac 15 C9
Krymskyy Pivostriv 17 B4
Kryvyy Rih 17 A4
Kuala Belait 23 C3
Kuala Lumpur 23 C2
Kuala Terengganu 23 C2
Kualakapuas 23 D3
Kuantan 23 C2
Kuban → 17 A5
Kuching 23 C3
Kudat 23 C3
Kugluktuk 36 C8
Kuichong 21 F11
Kulwin 32 C3
Kumagaya 22 E6
Kumai 23 D3
Kumamoto 22 G2
Kumanovo 15 C9
Kumara 33 K3
Kumasi 26 G5
Kumbakonam 25 D6
Kumbarilla 32 A5
Kumbia 32 A5
Kunlun Shan 20 C3
Kunming 20 D5
Kuopio 7 E9
Kupang 23 E4
Kuqa 20 B3
Kür → 17 C7
Kurdistan 24 B3
Kure 22 F3
Kurgan 18 D7
Kuril Is. = Kurilskiye Ostrova 19 E15
Kuril-Kamchatka Trench 34 C7
Kurilskiye Ostrova 19 E15
Kurnool 25 D6
Kurow 33 L3
Kurri Kurri 32 B5
Kursk 18 D4
Kuruktag 20 B3
Kuruman 29 K4
Kurume 22 G2
Kushiro 22 B9
Kuskokwim B. 36 D3
Kütahya 17 C4
Kutaisi 17 B6
Kuujjuaq 37 D13
Kuujjuarapik 37 D12
Kuwait ■ 24 C3
Kwajalein 34 G8
KwaMashu 29 K6
Kwango → 28 E3
Kwun Tong 21 G11
Kyabra Cr. → 32 A3
Kyabram 32 C4
Kyancutta 32 B2
Kyaukse 25 C8
Kyle of Lochalsh 10 D3
Kyneton 32 C3
Kyogle 32 A5
Kyōto 22 F4
Kyrgyzstan ■ 18 E8
Kythira 15 F10
Kyūshū 22 G2
Kyushu-Palau Ridge 34 F5
Kyyiv 18 D4
Kyzyl Kum 24 A5

L

La Barge 38 E8
La Belle 43 M5
La Ceiba 44 D7
La Coruña = A Coruña 13 A1
La Crescent 40 D9
La Crosse, Kans., U.S.A. 40 F5
La Crosse, Wis., U.S.A. 40 D9
La Désirade 44 b
La Fayette 43 H3
La Follette 43 G3
La Grande 38 D4
La Grande → 37 D12
La Grange, Ga., U.S.A. 43 J3
La Grange, Ky., U.S.A. 42 F3
La Grange, Tex., U.S.A. 41 L6
La Habana 44 B3
La Junta 41 F3
La Loche 36 D9
La Mancha 13 C4
La Mesa 39 K5
La Mesilla 39 K10
La Moure 40 B5
La Paz, Bolivia 46 G5
La Paz, Mexico 44 C2
La Perouse Str. 21 B9
La Pine 38 E3
La Plata 48 D5
La Porte 41 L7
La Push 38 C1
La Rioja □ 13 A4
La Roche-sur-Yon 12 C3
La Rochelle 12 C3
La Romana 45 D11
La Ronge 36 D9
La Salle 40 E10
La Spézia 12 D8
La Trinité 44 c
La Tuque 37 E12
La Vega 45 D10
La Vergne 43 G2
Labasa 33 C8
Labé 26 F3
Laborie 45 f
Labrador 37 D13
Labrador City 37 D13
Labrador Sea 37 D14
Labyrinth, L. 32 B2
Lac La Biche 36 D8
Lacepede B. 32 C2
Lacey 38 C2
Lachlan → 32 B3
Lackagh Hills 11 B3
Lacombe 36 D8
Laconia 42 D10
Ladozhskoye Ozero 7 E10
Ladysmith, S. Africa 29 K5
Ladysmith, U.S.A. 40 C9
Lae 30 B8
Lafayette, Ind., U.S.A. 42 E2
Lafayette, La., U.S.A. 41 K9
LaFayette, Tenn., U.S.A. 43 G2
Lagan → 11 B6
Lagos, Nigeria 26 G6
Lagos, Portugal 13 D1
Laguna 39 J10
Lahad Datu 23 C3
Lahat 23 D2
Lahn → 16 C3
Lahore 25 B6
Lahti 7 E9
Lairg 10 C4
Laizhou 21 C6
Lake 38 D8
Lake Andes 40 D5
Lake Arthur 41 K8
Lake Bindegolly △ 32 A3
Lake Cargelligo 32 B4
Lake Charles 41 K8
Lake City, Colo., U.S.A. 39 G10
Lake City, Fla., U.S.A. 43 K4
Lake City, Mich., U.S.A. 42 C3
Lake City, Minn., U.S.A. 40 C8
Lake City, S.C., U.S.A. 43 J6
Lake District △ 8 C4
Lake Eyre △ 32 A2
Lake Gairdner △ 32 B2
Lake Havasu City 39 J6
Lake Jackson 41 L7
Lake Mead △ 39 J6
Lake Meredith △ 41 H4
Lake Mills 40 D8
Lake Providence 41 J9
Lake Roosevelt △ 38 C4
Lake Torrens △ 32 B2
Lake Village 41 J9
Lake Wales 43 M5
Lake Worth 43 M5
Lakeba 33 D9
Lakeland 43 M5
Lakeport 38 G2
Lakes Entrance 32 C4
Lakeside 40 D3
Lakeview 38 E3
Lakeville 40 C8
Lakewood, Colo., U.S.A. 40 F2
Lakewood, Ohio, U.S.A. 42 E5
Lakin 41 G4
Lakota 40 A5
Lakshadweep Is. 25 E6
Lamar, Colo., U.S.A. 40 F3
Lamar, Mo., U.S.A. 41 G7
Lambay I. 11 C5
Lame Deer 38 D10
Lameroo 32 C3
Lamesa 41 J4
Lamington △ 32 A5
Lamma I. 21 G11
Lammermuir Hills 10 F6
Lamon B. 23 B4
Lamont 38 E10
Lampang 25 D8
Lampasas 41 K5
Lampeter 9 E3
Lamy 39 J11
Lanark 10 F5
Lancang Jiang → 20 D5
Lancashire □ 8 D5
Lancaster, U.K. 8 C5
Lancaster, Calif., U.S.A. 39 J4
Lancaster, Ky., U.S.A. 42 G3
Lancaster, N.H., U.S.A. 42 C10
Lancaster, Ohio, U.S.A. 42 F4
Lancaster, Pa., U.S.A. 42 E7
Lancaster, S.C., U.S.A. 43 H5
Lancaster, Wis., U.S.A. 40 D9
Lancaster Sd. 37 B11
Land Between the Lakes △ 43 G1
Lander 38 E9
Landes 12 D3
Land's End 9 G2
Lanett 43 J3
Langdon 40 A5
Langholm 10 F5
Langres 12 C6
Langres, Plateau de 12 C6
Langsa 23 C1
Langtry 41 L4
Languedoc 12 E5
Langwang 21 F9
Lannion 12 B2
Lansdowne 32 B5
L'Anse 42 B1
Lansing 42 D3
Lantau I. 21 G10
Lanzhou 20 C5
Lao Bao 23 B2
Laoag 23 B4
Laois □ 11 D4
Laon 12 B5
Laona 42 C1
Laos ■ 23 B2
Lapeer 42 D4
LaPorte 42 E2
Lappland 7 D8
Laptev Sea 19 B13
Laramie 40 E2
Laramie Mts. 40 E2
Laredo 41 M5
Largo 43 M4
Largs 10 F4
Larimore 40 B6
Larisa 15 E10
Larkana 24 C5
Larne 11 B6
Larned 40 F5
Larose 41 L9
Larrimah 30 D5
Larvik 7 F6
Las Animas 40 F3
Las Anod 24 E3
Las Cruces 39 K10
Las Palmas 26 C2
Las Tunas 45 C9
Las Vegas, N. Mex., U.S.A. 39 J11
Las Vegas, Nev., U.S.A. 39 H6
Lashio 25 C8
Lassen Pk. 38 F3
Lassen Volcanic △ 38 F3
Late 31 D16
Latina 14 D5
Latrobe 32 D4
Lau Basin 31 E15
Lau Fau Shan 21 G10
Lau Group 33 C9
Lau Ridge 31 E15
Laughlin 39 J6
Launceston, Australia 32 D4
Launceston, U.K. 9 G3
Laune → 11 D2
Laurel, Miss., U.S.A. 41 K10
Laurel, Mont., U.S.A. 38 D9
Laurencekirk 10 E6
Laurens 43 H4
Laurinburg 43 H6
Laurium 42 B1
Lausanne 12 C7
Laut 23 C2
Laut, Pulau 23 D3
Laut Kecil, Kepulauan 23 D3
Lautoka 33 C7
Lava Beds △ 38 F3
Lavagh More 11 B3
Laval 12 B3
Lawrence, N.Z. 33 L2
Lawrence, Ind., U.S.A. 42 F2
Lawrence, Kans., U.S.A. 40 F7
Lawrence, Mass., U.S.A. 42 D10
Lawrenceburg, Ind., U.S.A. 42 F3
Lawrenceburg, Tenn., U.S.A. 43 H2
Lawrenceville 43 J4
Lawton 41 H5
Laxford, L. 10 C3
Layla 24 C3
Layton 38 F7
Laytonville 38 G2
Lazio □ 14 C5
Le Creusot 12 C6
Le François 44 c
Le Gosier 44 b
Le Havre 12 B4
Le Lamentin 44 c
Le Mans 12 C4
Le Marin 44 c
Le Mars 40 D6
Le Moule 44 b
Le Prêcheur 44 c
Le Puy-en-Velay 12 D5
Le Robert 44 c
Le St-Esprit 44 c
Le Sueur 40 C8
Lea → 9 F8
Lead 40 C3
Leadville 39 G10
Leaf → 41 K10
Leamington 38 G7
Leane, L. 11 D2
Leatherhead 9 F7
Leavenworth, Kans., U.S.A. 40 F7
Leavenworth, Wash., U.S.A. 38 C3
Leawood 40 F7
Lebanon, Ind., U.S.A. 42 E2
Lebanon, Kans., U.S.A. 40 F5
Lebanon, Ky., U.S.A. 42 G3
Lebanon, Mo., U.S.A. 41 G8
Lebanon, N.H., U.S.A. 42 D9
Lebanon, Oreg., U.S.A. 38 D2
Lebanon, Pa., U.S.A. 42 E7
Lebanon, Tenn., U.S.A. 43 G2
Lebanon ■ 17 D5
Lebec 39 J4
Lecce 15 D8
Lee → 11 E3
Leech L. 40 B7
Leeds, U.K. 8 D6
Leeds, U.S.A. 43 J2
Leek 8 D5
Leesburg 43 L5
Leesville 41 K8
Leeton 32 B4
Leeuwarden 16 B2
Leeuwin, C. 30 G2
Leeward Is. 45 D12
Lefkada 15 E9
Leganés 13 B4
Legazpi 23 B4
Legnica 16 C8
Leh 25 B6
Lehigh Acres 43 M5
Leicester 9 E6
Leicestershire □ 9 E6
Leiden 16 B2
Leine → 16 B4
Leinster □ 11 C4
Leinster, Mt. 11 D5
Leipzig 16 C6
Leith 10 F5
Leith Hill 9 F7
Leitrim 11 B3
Leitrim □ 11 B4
Leizhou Bandao 21 D6
Leland, Mich., U.S.A. 42 C3
Leland, Miss., U.S.A. 41 J9
Léman, L. 12 C7
Lemhi Ra. 38 D7
Lemmon 40 C3
Lemoore 39 H4
Lena → 19 B13
Lenadoon Pt. 11 B2
Leninogorsk 18 D9
Leninsk-Kuznetskiy 18 D9
Lennox 40 D6
Lenoir 43 H5
Lenoir City 43 H3
Lens 12 A5
Leola 40 C5
Leominster, U.K. 9 E5
Leominster, U.S.A. 42 D10
León, Mexico 44 C4
León, Nic. 44 E7
León, Spain 13 A3
Leon, U.S.A. 40 E8
Leon → 41 K6
Leonardtown 42 F7
Leongatha 32 C4
Leonora 30 F3
Leoti 40 F4
Lerwick 10 A7
Les Cayes 45 D10
Les Sables-d'Olonne 12 C3
Lesbos 15 E12
Leshan 20 D5
Leskovac 15 C9
Lesotho ■ 29 K5
Lesser Antilles 45 E12
Lesser Slave L. 36 D8
Lesser Sunda Is. 23 D4
Leszno 16 C8
Letchworth 9 F7
Lethbridge 36 E8
Leti, Kepulauan 23 D4
Letterkenny 11 B4
Leuchars 10 E6
Leuven 16 C2
Levelland 41 J3
Leven 10 E6
Leven, L. 10 E5
Levin 33 J5
Lévis 37 E12
Levittown 42 E9
Lewes, U.K. 9 G8
Lewes, U.S.A. 42 F8
Lewis 10 C2
Lewis, Butt of 10 C2
Lewis Range 38 C7
Lewisburg, Tenn., U.S.A. 43 H2
Lewisburg, W. Va., U.S.A. 42 G5
Lewisporte 37 E14
Lewiston, Idaho, U.S.A. 38 C5
Lewiston, Maine, U.S.A. 43 C11
Lewistown, Mont., U.S.A. 38 C9
Lewistown, Pa., U.S.A. 42 E7
Lexington, Ill., U.S.A. 40 E10
Lexington, Ky., U.S.A. 42 F3
Lexington, Mo., U.S.A. 40 F8
Lexington, N.C., U.S.A. 43 H5
Lexington, Nebr., U.S.A. 40 E5
Lexington, Tenn., U.S.A. 43 H1
Lexington, Va., U.S.A. 42 G6
Lexington Park 42 F7
Leyburn 8 C6
Leyland 8 D5
Leyte □ 23 B4
Lhasa 20 D4
Lhazê 20 D3
L'Hospitalet de Llobregat 13 B7
Lianyungang 21 C6
Liaoning □ 21 B7
Liaoyang 21 B7
Liaoyuan 21 B7
Liard → 36 C7
Libby 38 B6
Liberal 41 G4
Liberec 16 C7
Liberia ■ 26 G4
Liberty, Mo., U.S.A. 40 F7
Liberty, N.Y., U.S.A. 42 E8
Liberty, Tex., U.S.A. 41 K7
Lībīya, Sahrâ' 27 C10
Libourne 12 D3
Libreville 28 D1
Libya ■ 27 C9
Lichfield 9 E6
Lichinga 29 G7
Licking → 42 F3
Liechtenstein ■ 12 C8
Liège 16 C2
Liepāja 18 D3
Liffey → 11 C5
Lifford 11 B4
Lifou, Î. 31 E12
Lightning Ridge 32 A4
Liguria □ 12 D8
Ligurian Sea 14 C3
Lijiang 20 D5
Likasi 28 G5
Lille 12 A5
Lillehammer 7 E6
Lilongwe 29 G6
Lima, Peru 46 F3
Lima, Mont., U.S.A. 38 D7
Lima, Ohio, U.S.A. 42 E3
Limavady 11 A5
Limbe 28 D1
Limeira 47 H9
Limerick 11 D3
Limerick □ 11 D3
Limfjorden 7 F5
Limnos 15 E11
Limoges 12 D4
Limón, Costa Rica 45 F8
Limon, U.S.A. 40 F3
Limousin □ 12 D4
Limoux 12 E5
Limpopo → 29 K6
Linares, Mexico 44 C5
Linares, Spain 13 C4
Lincoln, N.Z. 33 K4
Lincoln, U.K. 8 D7
Lincoln, Ill., U.S.A. 40 E10
Lincoln, Kans., U.S.A. 40 F5
Lincoln, Maine, U.S.A. 43 C11
Lincoln, N. Mex., U.S.A. 39 K11
Lincoln, Nebr., U.S.A. 40 E6
Lincoln City 38 D1
Lincoln Sea 6 A4
Lincolnshire □ 8 D7
Lincolnshire Wolds 8 D7
Lincolnton 43 H5
Lind 38 C4
Linden, Ala., U.S.A. 43 J2
Linden, Tex., U.S.A. 41 J7
Lindesnes 7 F5
Lindsay, Calif., U.S.A. 39 H4
Lindsay, Okla., U.S.A. 41 H6
Lindsborg 40 F6
Line Islands 35 H12
Lingding Yang 21 G10
Lingga, Kepulauan 23 D2
Lingle 40 D2
Linhai 21 D7
Linhares 47 G10
Linköping 7 F7
Linnhe, L. 10 E3
Linstead 44 a
Linton, Ind., U.S.A. 42 F2
Linton, N. Dak., U.S.A. 40 B4
Linxia 20 C5
Linz 16 D7
Lion, G. du 12 E6
Lipa 23 B4
Lipetsk 18 D4
Lippe → 16 C3
Lipscomb 41 G4
Liptrap, C. 32 C4
Liquillo, Sierra de 45 d
Lisboa 13 C1
Lisbon = Lisboa 13 C1
Lisbon 40 B6
Lisbon Falls 43 D10
Lisburn 11 B5
Liscannor B. 11 D2
Lisdoonvarna 11 C2
Lisianski I. 34 E10
Lisieux 12 B4
Lismore, Australia 32 A5
Lismore, Ireland 11 D4
Liston 32 A5
Listowel 11 D2
Litchfield, Ill., U.S.A. 40 F10
Litchfield, Minn., U.S.A. 40 C7
Lithgow 32 B5
Little Andaman I. 25 D8
Little Barrier I. 33 G5
Little Belt Mts. 38 C8
Little Bighorn Battlefield △ 38 D10
Little Blue → 40 F6
Little Colorado → 39 H8
Little Falls, Minn., U.S.A. 40 C7
Little Falls, N.Y., U.S.A. 42 D8
Little Fork → 40 A8
Little Humboldt → 38 F5
Little Minch 10 D2
Little Missouri → 40 B3
Little Ouse → 9 E9
Little Red → 41 H9
Little River 33 K4
Little Rock 41 H8
Little Sable Pt. 42 D2
Little Sioux → 40 E6
Little Snake → 38 F9
Little Wabash → 42 G1
Little White → 40 D4
Littlefield 41 J3
Littlehampton 9 G7
Littleton 42 C10
Liupanshui 20 D5
Liuzhou 21 D5
Live Oak 43 K4
Lively 42 B5
Livermore, Mt. 41 K2
Livermore Falls 43 C11
Liverpool, Canada 37 E13
Liverpool, U.K. 8 D4
Liverpool Bay 8 D4
Liverpool Ra. 32 B5
Livingston, U.K. 10 F5
Livingston, Ala., U.S.A. 43 J1
Livingston, Mont., U.S.A. 38 D8
Livingston, S.C., U.S.A. 43 J5
Livingston, Tenn., U.S.A. 43 G3
Livingston, Tex., U.S.A. 41 K7
Livingston, L. 41 K7
Livingstone 29 H5
Livonia 42 D4
Livorno 14 C4
Lizard Pt. 9 H2
Ljubljana 14 A6
Llandeilo 9 F4
Llandovery 9 F4
Llandrindod Wells 9 E4
Llandudno 8 D4
Llanelli 9 F3
Llangollen 8 E4
Llanidloes 9 E4
Llano 41 K5
Llano → 41 K5
Llano Estacado 41 J3
Llanos 46 C4
Llanwrtyd Wells 9 E4
Lleida 13 B6
Lleyn Peninsula 8 E3
Lloret de Mar 13 B7
Lloydminster 36 D9
Loa 39 G8
Lobatse 29 K5
Lobito 29 G2
Loch Lomond and the Trossachs △ 10 E4
Lochaber 10 E3
Locharbriggs 10 F5
Lochboisdale 10 D1
Loches 12 C4
Lochgilphead 10 E3
Lochinver 10 C3
Lochmaddy 10 D1
Lochnagar 10 E5
Lochy, L. 10 E4
Lock 32 B2
Lock Haven 42 E7
Lockerbie 10 F5
Lockhart 41 L6
Lockney 41 H4
Lockport 42 D6
Lodge Grass 38 D10
Lodgepole Cr. → 40 E2
Lodi 38 G3
Łódź 16 C9
Lofoten 7 D6
Logan, Iowa, U.S.A. 40 E7
Logan, Ohio, U.S.A. 42 F4
Logan, Utah, U.S.A. 38 F8
Logan, W. Va., U.S.A. 42 G5
Logan, Mt. 36 C5
Logansport, Ind., U.S.A. 42 E2
Logansport, La., U.S.A. 41 K8
Logroño 13 A4
Loir → 12 C3
Loire → 12 C2
Lolo 38 C6
Loma 38 C8
Lombárdia □ 12 D8
Lomblen 23 D4
Lombok 23 D3
Lomé 26 G6
Lomond, L. 10 E4
Lompoc 39 J3
London, Canada 37 E11
London, U.K. 9 F7
London, Ky., U.S.A. 42 G3
London, Ohio, U.S.A. 42 F4
London, Greater □ 9 F7
London Gatwick (LGW) 9 F7
London Heathrow (LHR) 9 F7
London Stansted (STN) 9 F8
Londonderry 11 B4
Londonderry □ 11 B4
Londonderry, C. 30 C4
Londrina 48 A6
Lone Pine 39 H4
Long B. 43 J6
Long Beach, Calif., U.S.A. 39 K4
Long Beach, Wash., U.S.A. 38 C1
Long Branch 42 E9
Long Creek 38 D4
Long Eaton 8 E6
Long I., Bahamas 45 C9
Long I., Ireland 11 E2
Long I., U.S.A. 42 E9
Long Island Sd. 42 E9
Long Lake 42 D8
Long Prairie 40 C7
Long Prairie → 40 C7
Long Xuyen 23 B2
Longbenton 8 B6
Longboat Key 43 M4
Longford, Australia 32 D4
Longford, Ireland 11 C4
Longford □ 11 C4
Longhua 21 F11
Longmont 40 E2
Longreach 30 E7
Longview, Tex., U.S.A. 41 J7
Longview, Wash., U.S.A. 38 C2
Longxue Dao 21 F10
Lonoke 41 H9
Lons-le-Saunier 12 C6
Looe 9 G3
Lookout, C. 43 H7
Loop Hd. 11 D2
Lop Nur 20 B4
Lopez, C. 28 E1
Lora Cr. → 32 A2
Lorain 42 E4
Lorca 13 D5
Lord Howe I. 31 G10
Lord Howe Rise 31 H12
Lord Howe Seamount Chain 31 F10
Lordsburg 39 K9
Lorient 12 C2
Lorn 10 E3
Lorn, Firth of 10 E3
Lorne 32 C3
Lorraine □ 12 B7
Los Alamos 39 J10
Los Angeles, Chile 48 D2
Los Angeles, U.S.A. 39 K4
Los Angeles Aqueduct 39 J5
Los Banos 39 H3
Los Lunas 39 J10
Los Mochis 44 B3
Lossiemouth 10 D5
Lostwithiel 9 G3
Lot → 12 D4
Loughborough 8 E6
Lougheed I. 37 B10
Loughrea 11 C3
Loughros More B. 11 B3
Louis Trichardt 29 J5
Louis XIV, Pte. 37 D12
Louisa 42 F4
Louisburgh 11 C2
Louisiade Arch. 30 C9
Louisiana 40 F9
Louisiana □ 41 K9
Louisville, Ky., U.S.A. 42 F3
Louisville, Miss., U.S.A. 41 J10
Louisville Ridge 34 L10
Loup City 40 E5
Lourdes 12 E3
Louth, Australia 32 B4
Louth, Ireland 11 C5
Louth, U.K. 8 D7
Louth □ 11 C5
Loveland 40 E2
Lovell 38 D9
Lovelock 38 F4
Loving 41 J2
Lovington 41 J3
Lowell 42 D10
Lower Alkali L. 38 F3
Lower California = Baja California 44 A1
Lower Hutt 33 J5
Lower Red L. 40 B7
Lower Saxony = Niedersachsen □ 16 B4
Lowestoft 9 E9
Lowville 42 D8
Loxton 32 B3
Loyauté, Îs. 31 E12
Lu Wo 21 F11
Lualaba → 28 D5
Luanda 28 F2
Luang Prabang 25 D9
Luanshya 29 G5
Luapula → 28 F5
Lubbock 41 J4
Lübeck 16 B5
Lublin 7 G8
Lubumbashi 29 G5
Lucania, Mt. 36 C5
Luce Bay 10 G4
Lucea 44 a
Lucedale 43 K1
Lucena 23 B4
Lucerne = Luzern 12 C8
Lucknow 25 C7
Lüda = Dalian 21 C7
Lüderitz 29 K3
Ludhiana 25 B6
Ludington 42 D2
Ludlow, U.K. 9 E5
Ludlow, U.S.A. 39 J5
Ludwigshafen 16 D4
Lufkin 41 K7
Lugano 12 C8
Lugh Ganana 24 E3
Lugnaquillia 11 D5
Lugo 13 A2
Luhansk 17 A5
Luing 10 E3
Luleå 7 D8
Luleälven → 7 D8
Luling 41 L6
Lumberton 43 H6
Lumsden 33 L2
Lundy 9 F3
Lune → 8 C5
Lüneburger Heide 16 B5
Lunéville 12 B7
Luni → 25 C6
Luning 38 G4
Luoyang 21 C6
Luray 42 F6
Lurgan 11 B5
Lusaka 29 H5
Lusk 40 D2
Lūt, Dasht-e 24 B4
Luton 9 F7
Łutselk'e 36 C8
Lutsk 18 D3
Luverne, Ala., U.S.A. 43 K2
Luverne, Minn., U.S.A. 40 D6
Luvua → 28 F5
Luxembourg 12 B7
Luxembourg ■ 12 B7
Luxi 20 D4
Luzern 12 C8
Luzhou 20 D5
Luzon 23 B4
Lviv 18 E3
Lyakhovskiye, Ostrova 19 B15
Lybster 10 C5
Lydenburg 29 K6
Lyell 33 J4
Lyman 38 F8
Lyme B. 9 G4
Lyme Regis 9 G5
Lymington 9 G6
Lynchburg 42 G6
Lynd Ra. 32 A4
Lynden 38 B2
Lyndhurst 32 B2
Lyndonville 42 C9
Lynn 42 D10
Lynn Haven 43 K3
Lynn Lake 36 D9
Lynton 9 F4
Lyon 12 D6
Lyonnais 12 D6
Lyons, Ga., U.S.A. 43 J4
Lyons, Kans., U.S.A. 40 F5
Lysychansk 17 A5
Lytham St. Anne's 8 D4
Lyttelton 33 K4

M

Ma'ān 24 B2
Ma'anshan 21 C6
Maas → 16 C2
Maastricht 12 A6
Mablethorpe 8 D8
McAlester 41 H7
McAllen 41 M5
MacAlpine L. 36 C9
Macapá 47 C8
Macau 21 G10
Macauley I. 31 G15
McCall 38 D5
McCamey 41 K3
McCammon 38 E7
Macclenny 43 K4
Macclesfield 8 D5
M'Clintock Chan. 36 B9
McCloud 38 F2
M'Clure Str. 37 B10
McClusky 40 B4
McComb 41 K9
McCook 40 E4
McDermitt 38 F5
McDonald Is. 5 G14
MacDonnell Ranges 30 E5
Macduff 10 D6
Macedonia □ 15 D10
Macedonia ■ 15 D9
Maceió 47 E11
Macfarlane, L. 32 B2
McGehee 41 J9
McGill 38 G6
Macgillycuddy's Reeks 11 E2
McGregor 40 D9
McGregor Ra. 32 A3
Machakos 28 E7
Machala 46 D3
Machias 43 C12
Machynlleth 9 E4
McIntosh 40 C4
Macintyre → 32 A5
Mackay, Australia 30 E8
Mackay, U.S.A. 38 E7
Mackay, L. 30 E4
McKeesport 42 E6
Mackenzie 36 D7
McKenzie 43 G1
Mackenzie → 36 C6
McKenzie → 38 D2
Mackenzie King I. 37 B10
Mackenzie Mts. 36 C7
Mackinaw City 42 C3
McKinley, Mt. 36 C4
McKinley Sea 6 A6
McKinney 41 J6
Macksville 32 B5
McLaughlin 40 C4
Maclean 32 A5
McLean 41 H4
McLeansboro 40 F10
Maclear 29 L5
Macleay → 32 B5
McLoughlin, Mt. 38 E2
McMinnville, Oreg., U.S.A. 38 D2
McMinnville, Tenn., U.S.A. 43 H3
McMurdo Sd. 6 E15
Macomb 40 E9
Mâcon, France 12 C6
Macon, Ga., U.S.A. 43 J4
Macon, Miss., U.S.A. 43 J1
Macon, Mo., U.S.A. 40 F8
McPherson 40 F6
McPherson Ra. 32 A5
Macquarie → 32 B4
Macquarie Harbour 32 D4
Macquarie Is. 34 N7
Macroom 11 E3
Macumba → 32 A2
Madadeni 29 K6
Madagascar ■ 29 J9
Madang 30 B8
Madeira 26 B2
Madeira → 46 D7
Madeleine, Îs. de la 37 E13
Madera 39 H3
Madhya Pradesh □ 25 C6
Madill 41 H6
Madīnat ash Sha'b 24 D3
Madison, Fla., U.S.A. 43 K4
Madison, Ind., U.S.A. 42 F3
Madison, Nebr., U.S.A. 40 E6
Madison, S. Dak., U.S.A. 40 D6
Madison, Wis., U.S.A. 40 D10
Madison → 38 D8
Madison Heights 42 G6
Madisonville, Ky., U.S.A. 42 G2
Madisonville, Tex., U.S.A. 41 K7
Madiun 23 D3
Madoc 42 C7
Madrakah, Ra's al 24 D4
Madras = Chennai 25 D7
Madras 38 D3
Madre, L. 41 M6
Madre de Dios → 46 F5
Madre de Dios, I. 48 G1
Madre Occidental, Sierra 44 B3
Madre Oriental, Sierra 44 C5
Madrid 13 B4
Madura 23 D3
Madurai 25 E6
Maebashi 22 E6
Maesteg 9 F4
Mafeking = Mafikeng 29 K5
Mafeteng 29 K5
Maffra 32 C4
Mafikeng 29 K5
Magadan 19 D16
Magallanes, Estrecho de 48 G2
Magdalena 39 J10
Magdalena → 46 A4
Magdeburg 16 B5
Magee 41 K10
Magelang 23 D3
Magellan's Str. = Magallanes, Estrecho de 48 G2
Maggiore, Lago 12 D8
Maggotty 44 a
Magherafelt 11 B5
Magnetic Pole (North) 37 B9
Magnetic Pole (South) 6 D13
Magnitogorsk 18 D6
Magnolia, Ark., U.S.A. 41 J8
Magnolia, Miss., U.S.A. 41 K9
Mahakam → 23 D3
Mahalapye 29 J5
Mahanadi → 25 C7
Maharashtra □ 25 C6
Maheno 33 L3
Mahia Pen. 33 H6
Mahilyow 18 D4
Mahinerangi, L. 33 L2
Mahnomen 40 B7
Maidenhead 9 F7
Maidstone 9 F8
Maiduguri 27 F8
Main →, Germany 16 D4
Main →, U.K. 11 B5
Main Range △ 32 A5
Maine 12 C3
Maine □ 43 C11
Maine → 11 D2
Mainland, Orkney, U.K. 10 C5
Mainland, Shet., U.K. 10 A7
Mainz 16 C4
Maitland, N.S.W., Australia 32 B5
Maitland, S. Austral., Australia 32 B2
Majorca = Mallorca 13 C7
Majuro 34 G9
Makale 23 D3
Makasar = Ujung Pandang 23 D3
Makasar, Selat 23 D3
Makgadikgadi Salt Pans 29 J5
Makhachkala 17 B7
Makiyivka 17 A5
Makkah 24 C2
Mal B. 11 D2
Malabar Coast 25 D6
Malacca, Straits of 23 C2
Malad City 38 E7
Málaga 13 D3
Malahide 11 C5
Malaita 31 B11
Malakula 31 D12
Malang 23 D3
Malanje 28 F3
Mälaren 7 F7
Malatya 17 C5
Malawi ■ 29 G6
Malawi, L. 29 G6
Malay Pen. 23 C2
Malaysia ■ 23 C3
Malbooma 32 B1
Malden 41 G10
Malden I. 35 H12
Maldives ■ 25 E6
Maldon 9 F8
Malebo, Pool 28 E3
Maleny 32 A5
Malheur → 38 D5
Malheur L. 38 E4
Mali ■ 26 E5
Malin Hd. 11 A4
Malin Pen. 11 A4
Mallacoota Inlet 32 C4
Mallaig 10 D3
Mallorca 13 C7
Mallow 11 D3
Malmö 7 F6
Malone 42 C8
Malpelo, I. de 35 G19
Malta, Idaho, U.S.A. 38 E7
Malta, Mont., U.S.A. 38 B10
Malta ■ 14 G6
Malton 8 C7
Maluku 23 D4
Malvern 41 H8
Malvern Hills 9 E5
Malvinas, Is. = Falkland Is. ☒ 48 G5
Mammoth 39 K8
Mammoth Cave △ 42 G3
Mamoré → 46 F5
Man, I. of 8 C3
Manado 23 C4
Managua 44 E7
Manapouri 33 L1
Manapouri, L. 33 L1
Manas 20 B3
Manassa 39 H11
Manatí 45 d
Manaus 46 D7
Manchester, U.K. 8 D5
Manchester, Ga., U.S.A. 43 J3
Manchester, Iowa, U.S.A. 40 D9
Manchester, Ky., U.S.A. 42 G4
Manchester, N.H., U.S.A. 42 D10
Manchester, Tenn., U.S.A. 43 H2
Manchester Int. (MAN) 8 D5
Manchuria = Dongbei 21 B7
Mandal 7 F5
Mandalay 25 C8
Mandan 40 B4
Mandeville 44 a
Mandsaur 25 C6
Mangaia 35 K12
Mangalore 25 D6
Mangaweka 33 H5
Mangnai 20 C4
Mangole 23 D4
Mangonui 33 F4
Mangum 41 H5
Manhattan 40 F6
Manicouagan → 37 E13
Manicouagan, Rés. 37 D13
Manihiki 35 J11
Manihiki Plateau 35 J11

Manila

Manila, Phil. 23 B4
Manila, U.S.A. 38 F9
Manila B. 23 B4
Manilla 32 B5
Manipur □ 25 C8
Manistee 42 C2
Manistee → 42 C2
Manistique 42 C2
Manitoba □ 36 D10
Manitoba, L. 36 D10
Manitou Is. 42 C2
Manitou Springs 40 F2
Manitoulin I. 37 E11
Manitowoc 42 C2
Manizales 46 B3
Mankato, Kans., U.S.A. 40 F5
Mankato, Minn., U.S.A. 40 C8
Mannahill 32 B3
Mannar 25 E6
Mannar, G. of 25 E6
Mannheim 16 D4
Manning, Canada 36 D8
Manning, U.S.A. 43 J5
Mannum 32 B2
Manokwari 23 D5
Manorhamilton 11 B3
Manosque 12 E6
Manra 31 A16
Mansel I. 37 C12
Mansfield, Australia 32 C4
Mansfield, U.K. 8 D6
Mansfield, La., U.S.A. 41 J8
Mansfield, Ohio, U.S.A. 42 E4
Mansfield, Tex., U.S.A. 41 J6
Mantalingajan, Mt. 23 C3
Manteca 39 H3
Manteo 43 H8
Mantes-la-Jolie 12 B4
Manti 38 G8
Manton 42 C3
Mántova 14 B4
Manu'a Is. 33 B14
Manukau 33 G5
Many 41 K8
Manzanillo, Cuba 45 C9
Manzanillo, Mexico 44 D4
Manzano Mts. 39 J10
Manzhouli 21 B6
Maoming 21 D6
Mapam Yumco 20 C3
Mapia, Kepulauan 23 C5
Mapleton 38 D2
Maputo 29 K6
Maquoketa 40 D9
Mar Chiquita, L. 48 C4
Mar del Plata 48 D5
Marabá 47 E9
Maracaibo 46 A4
Maracaibo, L. de 46 B4
Maracay 46 A5
Marajó, I. de 47 D9
Marana 39 K8
Maranoa → 32 A4
Marañón → 46 D4
Marathon 41 K3
Marbella 13 D3
Marble Falls 41 K5
March 9 E8
Marche 12 C4
Marco Island 43 N5
Mardan 25 B6
Maré, Î. 31 E12
Maree, L. 10 D3
Marengo 40 E8
Marfa 41 K2
Margarita, I. de 46 A6
Margate 9 F9
Mārgow, Dasht-e 24 B5
Maria I. 32 D4
Maria Island △ 32 D4
Maria van Diemen, C. 33 F4
Mariala △ 32 A4
Mariana Trench 34 F6
Marianna, Ark., U.S.A. 41 H9
Marianna, Fla., U.S.A. 43 K3
Marias → 38 C8
Maribor 14 A6
Maricopa, Ariz., U.S.A. 39 K7
Maricopa, Calif., U.S.A. 39 J4
Marie Byrd Land 6 E18
Marie-Galante 44 b
Mariental 29 J3
Marietta, Ga., U.S.A. 43 J3
Marietta, Ohio, U.S.A. 42 F5
Marília 47 H9
Marinette 42 C2
Maringá 48 A6
Marion, Ala., U.S.A. 43 J2
Marion, Ill., U.S.A. 41 G10
Marion, Ind., U.S.A. 42 E3
Marion, Iowa, U.S.A. 40 D9
Marion, Kans., U.S.A. 40 F6
Marion, N.C., U.S.A. 43 H5
Marion, Ohio, U.S.A. 42 E4
Marion, S.C., U.S.A. 43 H6
Marion, Va., U.S.A. 43 G5
Marion, L. 43 J5
Mariposa 39 H4
Maritimes, Alpes 12 D7
Mariupol 17 A5
Marked Tree 41 H9
Market Drayton 8 E5
Market Harborough 9 E7
Market Rasen 8 D7
Markham, Mt. 6 F15
Marksville 41 K8
Marla 32 A1
Marlborough 9 F6
Marlborough Downs 9 F6
Marlin 41 K6
Marlow, U.K. 9 F7
Marlow, U.S.A. 41 H6
Marmara Denizi 15 D13
Marne → 12 B5
Maroochydore 32 A5
Maroona 32 C3
Marquesas Fracture Zone 35 H15
Marquette 42 B2
Marquis 45 f
Marquises, Is. 35 H14
Marrakech 26 B4
Marrawah 32 D3
Marree 32 A2
Marrero 41 L9
Marrowie Cr. → 32 B4
Mars Hill 43 B12
Marsden 32 B4
Marseille 12 E6
Marsh I. 41 L9
Marshall, Ark., U.S.A. 41 H8
Marshall, Mich., U.S.A. 42 D3
Marshall, Minn., U.S.A. 40 C7
Marshall, Mo., U.S.A. 40 F8
Marshall, Tex., U.S.A. 41 J7
Marshall Is. ■ 34 G9
Marshalltown 40 D8
Marshfield, Mo., U.S.A. 41 G8
Marshfield, Wis., U.S.A. 40 C9
Mart 41 K6
Martaban, G. of 25 D8
Martapura 23 D3
Martha's Vineyard 42 E10
Martigues 12 E6
Martin, S. Dak., U.S.A. 40 D4
Martin, Tenn., U.S.A. 41 G10
Martin L. 43 J3
Martinborough 33 J5
Martinez 43 J4
Martinique ⊠ 44 c
Martin's Bay 45 g
Martins Ferry 42 E5
Martinsburg 42 F7
Martinsville, Ind., U.S.A. 42 F2
Martinsville, Va., U.S.A. 43 G6
Marton 33 J5
Maryborough, Queens., Australia 32 A5
Maryborough, Vic., Australia 32 C3
Maryland □ 42 F7
Maryport 8 C4
Marystown 37 E14
Marysville, Calif., U.S.A. 38 G3
Marysville, Kans., U.S.A. 40 F6
Marysville, Ohio, U.S.A. 42 E4
Maryville, Mo., U.S.A. 40 E7
Maryville, Tenn., U.S.A. 43 H4
Masan 21 C7
Masaya 44 E7
Masbate 23 B4
Maseru 29 K5
Mashhad 24 B4
Maşīrah 24 C4
Mask, L. 11 C2
Mason 41 K5
Mason City 40 D8
Masqat 24 C4
Massachusetts □ 42 D10
Massena 42 C8
Massiah Street 45 g
Massif Central 12 D5
Massillon 42 E5
Masterton 33 J5
Masvingo 29 J6
Mata Utu 31 C15
Matadi 28 F2
Matagalpa 44 E7
Matagami 37 E12
Matagami, L. 37 E12
Matagorda B. 41 L6
Matagorda I. 41 L6
Matamoros, Coahuila, Mexico 44 B5
Matamoros, Tamaulipas, Mexico 44 B5
Matane 37 E13
Matanzas 45 C8
Mataram 23 D3
Mataró 13 B7
Mataura 33 M2
Matehuala 44 C4
Matera 14 D7
Mathis 41 L6
Mathura 25 C6
Mati 23 C4
Matiri Ra. 33 J4
Matlock 8 D6
Mato Grosso □ 47 F8
Mato Grosso, Planalto do 47 G8
Matopo Hills 29 J5
Maţruḩ 24 C4
Matsue 22 F3
Matsumoto 22 E6
Matsusaka 22 F5
Matsuyama 22 G3
Mattagami → 37 D11
Mattancheri 25 E6
Matterhorn 12 D7
Matthew, Î. 31 E13
Mattoon 42 F1
Maturín 46 B6
Maubeuge 12 A6
Maubin 25 D8
Maude 32 B3
Maudin Sun 25 D8
Maughold Hd. 8 C3
Maumee 42 E4
Maumee → 42 E4
Maumere 23 D4
Maun 29 H4
Maupin 38 D3
Maurepas, L. 41 K9
Mauritania ■ 26 E3
Mauritius ■ 5 F13
Mauston 40 D9
Max 40 B4
May, C. 42 F8
May Pen 44 a
Mayaguana 45 C10
Mayagüez 45 d
Maybell 38 F9
Maybole 10 F4
Maydena 32 D4
Mayer 39 J7
Mayfield 43 G1
Mayhill 39 K11
Maykop 17 B6
Maynooth 11 C5
Mayo 36 C6
Mayo □ 11 C2
Mayor I. 33 G6
Maysville 42 F4
Mayville 40 B6
Mazār-e Sharīf 24 B5
Mazatlán 44 C3
Mazurski, Pojezierze 16 B10
Mbabane 29 K6
Mbandaka 28 D3
Mbanza Ngungu 28 F2
Mbeya 28 F6
Mbuji-Mayi 28 F4
McKean 31 A16
Mead, L. 39 H6
Meade 41 G4
Meadow Lake 36 D9
Meadow Valley Wash → 39 H6
Meadville 42 E5
Meares, C. 38 D2
Meath □ 11 C5
Meaux 12 B5
Mecca = Makkah 24 C2
Mechelen 16 C2
Mecklenburg 16 B5
Medan 23 C1
Médéa 26 A6
Medellín 46 B3
Medford, Oreg., U.S.A. 38 E2
Medford, Wis., U.S.A. 40 C9
Medicine Bow 38 F10
Medicine Bow Mts. 38 F10
Medicine Bow Pk. 38 F10
Medicine Hat 36 E8
Medicine Lake 40 A2
Medicine Lodge 41 G5
Medina = Al Madīnah 24 C2
Medina, N. Dak., U.S.A. 40 B5
Medina, N.Y., U.S.A. 42 D6
Medina, Ohio, U.S.A. 42 E5
Medina → 41 L5
Medina L. 41 L5
Mediterranean Sea 3 C11
Médoc 12 D3
Medway □ 9 F8
Medway → 9 F8
Meekatharra 30 F2
Meeker 38 F10
Meerut 25 C6
Meeteetse 38 D9
Meghalaya □ 25 C8
Mehlville 40 F9
Meighen I. 37 A10
Meiktila 25 C8
Meizhou 21 D6
Mekele 24 D2
Meknès 26 B4
Mekong → 23 C2
Melaka 23 C2
Melanesia 31 A10
Melanesian Basin 34 G8
Melbourne, Australia 32 C4
Melbourne, U.S.A. 43 L5
Mélèzes → 37 D12
Melfort 36 D9
Melitopol 17 A5
Mellen 40 B9
Mellette 40 C5
Melrose, Australia 32 B4
Melrose, U.K. 10 F6
Melrose, Minn., U.S.A. 40 C7
Melrose, N. Mex., U.S.A. 41 H3
Melstone 38 C10
Melton Mowbray 8 E7
Melun 12 B5
Melville 36 D9
Melville I., Australia 30 C5
Melville I., Canada 37 B9
Melville Pen. 37 C11
Melvin, Lough 11 B3
Memphis, Tenn., U.S.A. 41 H10
Memphis, Tex., U.S.A. 41 H4
Mena 41 H7
Menai Strait 8 D3
Menard 41 K5
Menard Fracture Zone 35 M18
Mendaña Fracture Zone 35 J18
Mende 12 D5
Mendip Hills 9 F5
Mendocino 38 G2
Mendocino, C. 38 F1
Mendocino Fracture Zone 35 D13
Mendota, Calif., U.S.A. 39 H3
Mendota, Ill., U.S.A. 40 E10
Mendoza 48 C3
Mengzi 20 D5
Menindee 32 B3
Menindee L. 32 B3
Meningie 32 C2
Menominee 42 C2
Menominee → 42 C2
Menomonie 40 C9
Menorca 13 C8
Mentawai, Kepulauan 23 D1
Mentor 42 E5
Merbein 32 B3
Merca 24 E3
Merced 39 H3
Mercer 33 G5
Mercy, C. 37 C13
Mere 9 F5
Meredith, L. 41 H4
Mergui 25 D8
Mérida, Mexico 44 C7
Mérida, Spain 13 C2
Mérida, Venezuela 46 B4
Mérida, Cord. de 46 B4
Meriden, U.K. 9 E6
Meriden, U.S.A. 42 E9
Meridian, Idaho, U.S.A. 38 E5
Meridian, Miss., U.S.A. 43 J1
Merkel 41 J5
Merrick 10 F4
Merrill, Oreg., U.S.A. 38 E3
Merrill, Wis., U.S.A. 40 C10
Merriman 40 D4
Merritt 36 D7
Merritt Island 43 L5
Merriwa 32 B5
Merryville 41 K8
Mersea I. 9 F8
Mersey → 8 D4
Merseyside □ 8 D4
Mersin = İçel 17 C4
Merthyr Tydfil 9 F4
Mertzon 41 K4
Mesa 39 K8
Mesa Verde △ 39 H9
Mesopotamia = Al Jazirah 24 B3
Mesquite 39 H6
Messina 14 E6
Messina, Str. di 14 F6
Meta → 46 B5
Meta Incognita Pen. 37 C13
Metairie 41 L9
Metaline Falls 38 B5
Methven 33 K3
Metlakatla 36 D6
Metropolis 41 G10
Metz 12 B7
Meuse → 12 A6
Mexia 41 K6
Mexicali 44 A1
Mexican Water 39 H9
México, Mexico 44 D5
Mexico, U.S.A. 40 F9
Mexico ■ 44 C4
México, Ciudad de 44 D5
Mexico, G. of 44 C7
Meymaneh 24 B5
Mezen → 18 C5
Miami, Fla., U.S.A. 43 N5
Miami, Okla., U.S.A. 41 G7
Miami, Tex., U.S.A. 41 H4
Miami Beach 43 N5
Mianwali 25 B6
Miass 18 D7
Michigan □ 42 C3
Michigan, L. 42 D2
Michigan City 42 E2
Michurinsk 18 D5
Micoud 45 f
Micronesia 34 G7
Micronesia, Federated States of ■ 34 G7
Mid-Pacific Seamounts 34 F10
Middelburg 29 L5
Middle Alkali L. 38 F3
Middle East 24 B2
Middle Loup → 40 E5
Middleburg 43 K5
Middlebury 42 C9
Middleport 42 F4
Middlesboro 43 G4
Middlesbrough 8 C6
Middletown, U.K. 11 B5
Middletown, N.Y., U.S.A. 42 E8
Middletown, Ohio, U.S.A. 42 F3
Midhurst 9 G7
Midi, Canal du → 12 E4
Midland, Mich., U.S.A. 42 D3
Midland, Tex., U.S.A. 41 K3
Midleton 11 E3
Midlothian □ 10 F5
Midway Is. 34 E10
Midwest 38 E10
Midwest City 41 H6
Mieres 13 A3
Milaca 40 C8
Milan, Mo., U.S.A. 40 E8
Milan, Tenn., U.S.A. 43 H1
Milano 12 D8
Milbank 40 C6
Mildenhall 9 E8
Mildura 32 B3
Miles 32 A5
Miles City 40 B2
Milford, Del., U.S.A. 42 F8
Milford, Utah, U.S.A. 39 G7
Milford Haven 9 F2
Milford Sd. 33 L1
Milford Sound 33 L1
Millau 12 D5
Millbrook 43 J2
Mille Lacs L. 40 B8
Milledgeville 43 J4
Millen 43 J5
Millennium I. = Caroline I. 35 H12
Miller 40 C5
Millet 45 f
Millicent 32 C3
Millington 41 H10
Millinocket 43 C11
Millmerran 32 A5
Millom 8 C4
Millstreet 11 D2
Milltown Malbay 11 D2
Millville 42 F8
Millwood L. 41 J8
Milo 43 C11
Milparinka 32 A3
Milton, N.Z. 33 M2
Milton, Fla., U.S.A. 43 K2
Milton, Pa., U.S.A. 42 E7
Milton-Freewater 38 D4
Milton Keynes 9 E7
Milwaukee 42 D2
Milwaukee Deep 2 D6
Milwaukie 38 D2
Min Jiang →, Fujian, China 21 D6
Min Jiang →, Sichuan, China 20 D5
Minami-Tori-Shima 34 E7
Minas Gerais □ 47 G9
Minatitlán 44 D6
Minbu 25 C8
Mindanao 23 C4
Mindanao Trench 23 B4
Minden, La., U.S.A. 41 J8
Minden, Nev., U.S.A. 38 G4
Mindoro 23 B4
Mindoro Str. 23 B4
Minehead 9 F4
Mineola 41 J7
Mineral Wells 41 J5
Minidoka 38 E7
Minneapolis, Kans., U.S.A. 40 F6
Minneapolis, Minn., U.S.A. 40 C8
Minnesota □ 40 B8
Minnesota → 40 C8
Minnewaukan 40 A5
Minnipa 32 B2
Minorca = Menorca 13 C8
Minot 40 A4
Minsk 18 D3
Mintabie 32 A1
Minto, L. 37 D12
Minturn 38 G10
Minzhong 21 F10
Miramichi 37 E13
Mirbāţ 24 D4
Miri 23 C3
Mirjāveh 24 C5
Mirzapur 25 C7
Mishan 21 B8
Mishawaka 42 E2
Misool 23 D5
Mişrātah 27 B9
Missinaibi → 37 D11
Mission, S. Dak., U.S.A. 40 D4
Mission, Tex., U.S.A. 41 M5
Mission Viejo 39 K5
Mississippi □ 41 J10
Mississippi → 41 L10
Mississippi River Delta 41 L9
Mississippi Sd. 41 K10
Missoula 38 C7
Missouri □ 40 F8
Missouri → 40 F9
Missouri City 41 L7
Missouri Valley 40 E7
Mistassini, L. 37 D12
Mitchell, Australia 32 A4
Mitchell, Nebr., U.S.A. 40 E3
Mitchell, Oreg., U.S.A. 38 D3
Mitchell, S. Dak., U.S.A. 40 D6
Mitchell → 30 D7
Mitchell, Mt. 43 H4
Mitchelstown 11 D3
Mito 22 E7
Mitsiwa 24 D2
Mittagong 32 B5
Mitumba, Mts. 28 F5
Miyakonojō 22 H2
Miyazaki 22 H2
Mizen Hd., Cork, Ireland 11 E2
Mizen Hd., Wicklow, Ireland 11 D5
Mizoram □ 25 C8
Mjøsa 7 E6
Mmabatho 29 K5
Mo i Rana 7 D6
Moa, I. 30 C7
Moab 39 G9
Moala 33 D8
Moama 32 C3
Moate 11 C4
Moberly 40 F8
Mobile 43 K1
Mobile B. 43 K2
Mobridge 40 C4
Mochudi 29 J5
Moclips 38 C1
Módena, Italy 14 B4
Modena, U.S.A. 39 H7
Modesto 39 H3
Modimolle 29 J5
Moe 32 C4
Moffat 10 F5
Mogadishu = Muqdisho 24 E3
Mogi das Cruzes 48 A7
Mogollon Rim 39 J8
Mohall 40 A4
Mohave, L. 39 J6
Moher, Cliffs of 11 D2
Moidart, L. 10 E3
Moisie → 37 D13
Mojave 39 J4
Mojave △ 39 J6
Mojave Desert 39 J5
Mokai 33 H5
Mokau 33 H5
Mokopane 29 J5
Mold 8 D4
Moldavia = Moldova ■ 17 A3
Molde 7 E5
Moldova ■ 17 A3
Mole → 9 F7
Mole Creek 32 D4
Molepolole 29 J5
Moline 40 E9
Mollendo 46 G4
Molokai Fracture Zone 35 E15
Molong 32 B4
Molopo → 29 K4
Molucca Sea 23 D4
Moluccas = Maluku 23 D4
Mombasa 28 E7
Mona Passage 45 D11
Monaco ■ 12 E7
Monadhliath Mts. 10 D4
Monaghan 11 B5
Monaghan □ 11 B5
Monahans 41 K3
Monar, L. 10 D3
Monasterevin 11 C4
Mönchengladbach 16 C3
Moncks Corner 43 J5
Monclova 44 B4
Moncton 37 E13
Mondeodo 23 D4
Moneague 44 a
Monessen 42 E6
Monett 41 G8
Moneymore 11 B5
Mongolia ■ 20 B5
Mongu 29 H4
Monifieth 10 E6
Monmouth, U.K. 9 F5
Monmouth, Ill., U.S.A. 40 E9
Monmouth, Oreg., U.S.A. 38 D2
Monmouthshire □ 9 F5
Mono L. 39 H4
Monroe, Ga., U.S.A. 43 J4
Monroe, La., U.S.A. 41 J8
Monroe, Mich., U.S.A. 42 E4
Monroe, N.C., U.S.A. 43 H5
Monroe, Utah, U.S.A. 39 G7
Monroe, Wis., U.S.A. 40 D10
Monroe City 40 F9
Monroeville 43 K2
Monrovia 26 G3
Mons 16 C1
Mont-de-Marsan 12 E3
Mont-Laurier 37 E12
Montana □ 38 C9
Montargis 12 C5
Montauban 12 D4
Montauk Pt. 42 E10
Montbéliard 12 C7
Montceau-les-Mines 12 C6
Monte-Carlo 12 E7
Monte Cristi 45 D10
Monte Vista 39 H10
Montego Bay 44 a
Montélimar 12 D6
Montello 40 D10
Montemorelos 44 B5
Montenegro ■ 15 C8
Monterey 39 H3
Montería 46 B3
Monterrey 44 B4
Montes Claros 47 G10
Montesano 38 C2
Montevideo, Uruguay 48 C5
Montevideo, U.S.A. 40 C7
Montezuma 40 E8
Montezuma Castle △ 39 J8
Montgomery, U.K. 9 E4
Montgomery, Ala., U.S.A. 43 J2
Montgomery, W. Va., U.S.A. 42 F5
Montgomery City 40 F9
Monticello, Ark., U.S.A. 41 J9
Monticello, Fla., U.S.A. 43 K4
Monticello, Ind., U.S.A. 42 E2
Monticello, Iowa, U.S.A. 40 D9
Monticello, Ky., U.S.A. 43 G3
Monticello, Minn., U.S.A. 40 C8
Monticello, Miss., U.S.A. 41 K9
Monticello, Utah, U.S.A. 39 H9
Montluçon 12 C5
Montpelier, Idaho, U.S.A. 38 E8
Montpelier, Vt., U.S.A. 42 C9
Montpellier 12 E5
Montréal 37 E12
Montreux 12 C7
Montrose, U.K. 10 E6
Montrose, U.S.A. 39 G10
Montserrat ⊠ 45 D12
Monywa 25 C8
Monza 12 D8
Monze 29 H5
Moonie 32 A5
Moonie → 32 A4
Moonta 32 B2
Moorcroft 40 C2
Moorefield 42 F6
Moorfoot Hills 10 F5
Moorhead 40 B6
Moorreesburg 29 L3
Moose Jaw 36 D9
Moose Lake 40 B8
Moosehead L. 43 C11
Mooselookmeguntic L. 43 C10
Moosomin 36 D9
Moosonee 37 D11
Mopti 26 F5
Mora, Sweden 7 E6
Mora, Minn., U.S.A. 40 C8
Mora, N. Mex., U.S.A. 39 J11
Moradabad 25 C6
Moran, Kans., U.S.A. 41 G7
Moran, Wyo., U.S.A. 38 E8
Morant Bay 44 a
Morant Pt. 44 a
Morar, L. 10 E3
Moratuwa 25 E6
Morava →, Serbia 15 B9
Morava →, Slovak Rep. 16 D8
Moray □ 10 D5
Moray Firth 10 D5
Morden 36 E10
Moreau → 40 C4
Morecambe 8 C5
Morecambe B. 8 C5
Moree 32 A4
Morehead 42 F4
Morehead City 43 H7
Morelia 44 D4
Morena, Sierra 13 C3
Moresby I. 36 D6
Moreton I. 32 A5
Moreton Island △ 32 A5
Morgan 38 F8
Morgan City 41 L9
Morganfield 42 G2
Morganton 43 H5
Morgantown 42 F6
Moriarty 39 J10
Morioka 22 D7
Morlaix 12 B2
Mornington 32 C4
Moro G. 23 C4
Morocco ■ 26 B4
Morogoro 28 F7
Morón 45 C9
Moroni 38 G8
Morotai 23 C4
Morpeth 8 B6
Morrilton 41 H8
Morrinsville 33 G5
Morris, Ill., U.S.A. 40 E10
Morris, Minn., U.S.A. 40 C7
Morristown, Ariz., U.S.A. 39 K7
Morristown, Tenn., U.S.A. 43 G4
Morro Bay 39 J3
Mortlake 32 C3
Morton, Tex., U.S.A. 41 J3
Morton, Wash., U.S.A. 38 C2
Morundah 32 B4
Moruya 32 C5
Morven 32 A4
Morvern 10 E3
Morwell 32 C4
Moscow = Moskva 18 D4
Moscow 38 C5
Mosel → 12 A7
Moses Lake 38 C4
Mosgiel 33 L3
Moshi 28 E7
Moskva 18 D4
Mosquero 41 H3
Moss Vale 32 B5
Mossburn 33 L2
Mosselbaai 29 L4
Mossgiel 32 B3
Mossoró 47 E11
Most 16 C6
Mostaganem 26 A6
Mostar 15 C7
Mosul = Al Mawşil 24 B3
Motherwell 10 F5
Mott 40 B3
Motueka 33 J4
Motueka → 33 J4
Moulamein 32 C3
Moule à Chique, C. 45 f
Moulins 12 C5
Moulmein 25 D8
Moultrie 43 K4
Moultrie, L. 43 J5
Mound City, Mo., U.S.A. 40 E7
Mound City, S. Dak., U.S.A. 40 C4
Moundsville 42 F5
Mount Airy 43 G5
Mount Aspiring △ 33 L2
Mount Barker 32 C2
Mount Bellew Bridge 11 C3
Mount Burr 32 C3
Mount Carmel 42 F2
Mount Desert I. 43 C11
Mount Dora 43 L5
Mount Field △ 32 D4
Mount Gambier 32 C3
Mount Hagen 30 B7
Mount Hope, N.S.W., Australia 32 B4
Mount Hope, S. Austral., Australia 32 B2
Mount Isa 30 E6
Mount Kaputar △ 32 B5
Mount Lofty Ranges 32 B2
Mount Magnet 30 F2
Mount Maunganui 33 G6
Mount Perry 32 A5
Mount Pleasant, Iowa, U.S.A. 40 E9
Mount Pleasant, Mich., U.S.A. 42 D3
Mount Pleasant, S.C., U.S.A. 43 J6
Mount Pleasant, Tenn., U.S.A. 43 H2
Mount Pleasant, Tex., U.S.A. 41 J7
Mount Pleasant, Utah, U.S.A. 38 G8
Mount Rainier △ 38 C3
Mount St. Helens △ 38 C2
Mount Shasta 38 F2
Mount Sterling, Ill., U.S.A. 40 F9
Mount Sterling, Ky., U.S.A. 42 F4
Mount Vernon, Ill., U.S.A. 42 F1
Mount Vernon, Ind., U.S.A. 40 F10
Mount Vernon, Ohio, U.S.A. 42 E4
Mount Vernon, Wash., U.S.A. 38 B2
Mount William △ 32 D4
Mountain Ash 9 F4
Mountain City, Nev., U.S.A. 38 F6
Mountain City, Tenn., U.S.A. 43 G5
Mountain Grove 41 G8
Mountain Home, Ark., U.S.A. 41 G8
Mountain Home, Idaho, U.S.A. 38 E6
Mountain Iron 40 B8
Mountain View 41 H8
Mountainair 39 J10
Mountmellick 11 C4
Mountrath 11 D4
Mourne → 11 B4
Mourne Mts. 11 B5
Moville 11 A4
Moy → 11 B2
Moyen Atlas 26 B4
Mozambique ■ 29 H7
Mozambique Chan. 3 E13
Mpumalanga 29 K6
Mthatha 29 L5
Mu Us Shamo 21 C5
Muar 23 C2
Muck 10 E2
Muckadilla 32 A4
Muckle Flugga 10 A8
Mudanjiang 21 B7
Muddy Cr. → 39 H8
Mudgee 32 B4
Mufulira 29 G5
Muhammad Qol 24 C2
Mui Wo 21 G10
Muine Bheag 11 D5
Muir of Ord 10 D4
Mulde → 16 C6
Mule Creek Junction 40 D2
Muleshoe 41 H3
Mulhacén 13 D4
Mulhouse 12 C7
Mull 10 E3
Mull, Sound of 10 E3
Mullen 40 D4
Mullens 42 G5
Muller, Pegunungan 23 C3
Mullet Pen. 11 B1
Mullingar 11 C4
Mullins 43 H6
Mullumbimby 32 A5
Mulroy B. 11 A4
Multan 25 B6
Mulvane 41 G6
Mumbai 25 D6
Muna 23 D4
München 16 D5
Muncie 42 E3
Mundabbera 32 A5
Munday 41 J5
Mungallala 32 A4
Mungallala Cr. → 32 A4
Munich = München 16 D5
Munising 42 B2
Münster 16 C3
Munster □ 11 D3
Muong Sai 23 A2
Muqdisho 24 E3
Murchison → 30 F1
Murcia 13 D5
Murdo 40 D4
Mureş → 17 A2
Murfreesboro, N.C., U.S.A. 43 G7
Murfreesboro, Tenn., U.S.A. 43 H2
Murgon 32 A5
Müritz 16 B6
Murmansk 7 D10
Murom 18 D5
Murphy 38 E5
Murray, Ky., U.S.A. 43 G1
Murray, Utah, U.S.A. 38 F8
Murray → 32 C2
Murray, L. 43 H5
Murray Bridge 32 C2
Murray Fracture Zone 35 D14
Murray River △ 32 B3
Murrumbidgee → 32 B3
Murrumburrah 32 B4
Murrurundi 32 B5
Murtoa 32 C3
Mururoa 35 K14
Murwillumbah 32 A5
Mûsa, Gebel 27 C12
Muscat = Masqat 24 C4
Muscatine 40 E9
Muscle Shoals 43 H2
Musgrave Ranges 30 F5
Musi → 23 D2
Musina 29 J6
Muskegon 42 D2
Muskegon → 42 D2
Muskegon Heights 42 D2
Muskogee 41 H7
Musselburgh 10 F5
Musselshell → 38 C10
Muswellbrook 32 B5
Mutare 29 H6
Mutton I. 11 D2
Mwanza 28 E6
Mweelrea 11 C2
Mweru, L. 28 F5
My Tho 23 B2
Myanmar = Burma ■ 25 C8
Myeik Kyunzu 25 D8
Myingyan 25 C8
Myitkyina 25 C8
Mykolayiv 17 A4
Mynydd Du 9 F4
Myrtle Beach 43 J6
Myrtle Creek 38 E2
Myrtle Point 38 E1
Mysore 25 D6

N

Naab → 16 D6
Naas 11 C5
Naberezhnyye Chelny 18 D6
Naches 38 C3
Nacimiento, L. 39 J3
Nacogdoches 41 K7
Nacozari de García 44 A3
Nadi 33 C7
Naga 23 B4
Nagaland □ 25 C8
Nagano 22 E6
Nagaoka 22 E6
Nagasaki 22 G1
Nagercoil 25 E6
Nagles Mts. 11 D3
Nagoya 22 F5
Nagpur 25 C6
Naguabo 45 d
Naha 21 D7
Nain 37 D13
Nairn 10 D5
Nairobi 28 E7
Najd 24 C3
Najrān 24 D3
Nakhodka 19 E14
Nakhon Ratchasima 23 B2
Nakhon Sawan 25 D9
Nakhon Si Thammarat 23 C2
Nakina 37 D11
Nakuru 28 E7
Nalchik 17 B6
Nam Co 20 C4
Nam Dinh 23 A2
Namaland 29 K3
Namangan 18 E8
Nambour 32 A5
Nambucca Heads 32 B5
Namcha Barwa 20 D4
Namib Desert 29 J3
Namibe 29 H2
Namibia ■ 29 J3
Namlea 23 D4
Namoi → 32 B4
Nampa 38 E5
Namp'o 21 C7
Nampula 29 H7
Namumea 31 B14
Namur 16 C2
Nanaimo 36 E7
Nanango 32 A5
Nanchang 21 D6
Nanchong 20 C5
Nancy 12 B7
Nanded 25 D6
Nandewar Ra. 32 B5
Nanjing 21 C6
Nanking = Nanjing 21 C6
Nanlang 21 G10
Nanning 20 D5
Nanping 21 D6
Nansen Sd. 37 B9
Nansha 21 F10
Nantes 12 C3
Nanticoke 42 E7
Nantong 21 C7
Nantou 21 F10
Nantucket I. 42 E10
Nantwich 8 D5
Nanumanga 31 B14
Nanusa, Kepulauan 23 C4
Nanyang 21 C6
Napa 38 G2
Napier 33 H6
Naples = Nápoli 14 D6
Naples 43 M5
Napo → 46 D4
Napoleon, N. Dak., U.S.A. 40 B5
Napoleon, Ohio, U.S.A. 42 E3
Nápoli 14 D6
Nara Visa 41 H3
Naracoorte 32 C3
Naradhan 32 B4
Narberth 9 F3
Narbonne 12 E5
Narmada → 25 C6
Narooma 32 C5
Narrabri 32 B4
Narran → 32 A4
Narrandera 32 B4
Narromine 32 B4
Narvik 7 D7
Naryn 25 A6
Naseby 33 L3
Naser, Buheirat en 27 D12
Nashua, Mont., U.S.A. 38 B10
Nashua, N.H., U.S.A. 42 D10
Nashville, Ark., U.S.A. 41 J8
Nashville, Ga., U.S.A. 43 K4
Nashville, Tenn., U.S.A. 43 G2
Nasik 25 D6
Nassau 45 B9
Natal 47 E11
Natashquan 37 D13
Natashquan → 37 D13
Natchez 41 K9
Natchitoches 41 K8
Nathalia 32 C4
Natimuk 32 C3
Natuna Besar, Kepulauan 23 C2
Natuna Selatan, Kepulauan 23 C2
Natural Bridges △ 39 H8
Naturaliste, C. 32 D4
Naturaliste Plateau 30 G1
Nauru ■ 34 H8
Navajo Res. 39 H10
Navarra □ 13 A5
Navasota 41 K6
Naver → 10 C4
Navojoa 44 B3
Nawabshah 24 C5
Nawoiy 24 A5
Naxos 15 F11
Nazas → 44 B4
Nazca Ridge 35 K19
Naze, The 9 F9
Ndjamena 27 F8
Ndola 29 G5
Neagh, Lough 11 B5
Neah Bay 38 B1
Neales → 32 A2
Near Is. 36 D1
Neath 9 F4
Nebine Cr. → 32 A4
Nebraska □ 40 E5
Nebraska City 40 E7
Necedah 40 C9
Neches → 41 L8
Neckar → 16 D4
Needles 39 J6
Needles, The 9 G6
Neenah 42 C1
Neepawa 36 D10
Nefyn 8 E3
Negaunee 42 B2
Negril 44 a
Negro →, Argentina 48 E4
Negro →, Brazil 46 D7
Negros 23 C4
Nei Monggol Zizhiqu □ 21 B6
Neijiang 20 D5
Neilingding Dao 21 G10
Neillsville 40 C9
Neilton 38 C2
Neiva 46 C3
Neligh 40 D6
Nellore 25 D6
Nelson, Canada 36 E8
Nelson, N.Z. 33 J4
Nelson, U.K. 8 D5
Nelson, U.S.A. 39 J7
Nelson → 36 D10
Nelson, C. 32 C3
Nelson Lakes △ 33 J4
Nelspruit 29 K6
Nemunas → 18 D3
Nen Jiang → 21 B7
Nenagh 11 D3
Nendo 31 C12
Nene → 9 E8
Nenjiang 21 B7
Neodesha 41 G7
Neosho 41 G7
Neosho → 41 H7
Nepal ■ 25 C7
Nephi 38 G8
Nephin 11 B2
Nephin Beg Range 11 C2
Nerang 32 A5
Ness, L. 10 D4
Ness City 40 F5
Netherlands ■ 16 C2
Netherlands Antilles ⊠ 45 E11
Nettilling L. 37 C12
Neuchâtel 12 C7
Neuchâtel, Lac de 12 C7
Neuse → 43 H7
Neusiedler See 16 E8
Neva → 7 E10
Nevada, Iowa, U.S.A. 40 D8
Nevada, Mo., U.S.A. 41 G7
Nevada □ 38 G5
Nevada City 38 G3
Nevers 12 C5
Nevertire 32 B4
Nevinnomyssk 17 B6
New → 42 F5
New Albany, Ind., U.S.A. 42 F3
New Albany, Miss., U.S.A. 41 H10
New Amsterdam 46 B7
New Angledool 32 A4
New Baltimore 42 D4
New Bedford 42 E10
New Bern 43 H7
New Boston 41 J7
New Braunfels 41 L5
New Brighton 33 K4
New Britain, Papua N. G. 30 B9
New Britain, U.S.A. 42 E9
New Britain Trench 30 J3
New Brunswick 42 E8
New Brunswick □ 37 E13
New Caledonia ⊠ 31 E12
New Caledonia Trough 34 L8
New Castle, Ind., U.S.A. 42 F3
New Castle, Pa., U.S.A. 42 E5
New Delhi 25 C6
New England 40 B3
New England Ra. 32 B5
New Forest 9 G6
New Galloway 10 F4
New Georgia Is. 31 B10
New Glasgow 37 E13
New Guinea 30 B7
New Hampshire □ 42 D10
New Hampton 40 D8
New Haven 42 E9
New Hebrides = Vanuatu ■ 31 D12
New Iberia 41 K9
New Ireland 30 A9
New Jersey □ 42 E8
New Lexington 42 F4
New Liskeard 37 E12
New London, Conn., U.S.A. 42 E9
New London, Wis., U.S.A. 40 C10
New Madrid 41 G10
New Martinsville 42 F5
New Meadows 38 D5
New Mexico □ 39 J10
New Norfolk 32 D4
New Orleans 41 L9
New Philadelphia 42 E5
New Plymouth, N.Z. 33 H5
New Plymouth, U.S.A. 38 E5
New Port Richey 43 L4
New Providence 45 B9
New Quay 9 E3
New Radnor 9 E4
New Richmond 40 C8
New River Gorge △ 42 G5
New Roads 41 K9
New Rockford 40 B5
New Romney 9 G8
New Ross 11 D5
New Salem 40 B4
New Smyrna Beach 43 L5
New South Wales □ 32 B4
New Tecumseth 42 C6
New Town 40 B3
New Tredegar 9 F4
New Ulm 40 C7
New Westminster 38 B2
New York 42 E9
New York □ 42 D8
New Zealand ■ 33 J6
Newark, Del., U.S.A. 42 F8
Newark, N.J., U.S.A. 42 E8
Newark, N.Y., U.S.A. 42 D7
Newark, Ohio, U.S.A. 42 E4
Newark-on-Trent 8 D7
Newberg 38 D2
Newberry, Mich., U.S.A. 42 B3
Newberry, S.C., U.S.A. 43 H5
Newburgh 42 E8
Newbury 9 F6
Newburyport 43 D10
Newcastle, Australia 32 B5
Newcastle, S. Africa 29 K5
Newcastle, U.K. 11 B6
Newcastle, U.S.A. 40 D2
Newcastle Emlyn 9 E3
Newcastle-under-Lyme 8 D5
Newcastle-upon-Tyne 8 C6
Newcastle West 11 D2
Newell 40 C3
Newfoundland & Labrador □ 37 D14
Newhaven 9 G8
Newkirk 41 G6
Newlyn 9 G2
Newman 30 E2
Newmarket, Ireland 11 D2
Newmarket, U.K. 9 E8
Newnan 43 J3
Newport, Ireland 11 C2
Newport, I. of W., U.K. 9 G6
Newport, Newport, U.K. 9 F5
Newport, Ark., U.S.A. 41 H9
Newport, Ky., U.S.A. 42 F3
Newport, N.H., U.S.A. 42 D9
Newport, Oreg., U.S.A. 38 D1
Newport, R.I., U.S.A. 42 E10
Newport, Tenn., U.S.A. 43 H4
Newport, Vt., U.S.A. 42 C9
Newport, Wash., U.S.A. 38 B5
Newport Beach 39 K5
Newport News 42 G7
Newport Pagnell 9 E7
Newquay 9 G2
Newry 11 B5
Newton, Ill., U.S.A. 40 F10
Newton, Iowa, U.S.A. 40 E8
Newton, Kans., U.S.A. 41 F6
Newton, Mass., U.S.A. 42 D10
Newton, Miss., U.S.A. 41 J10
Newton, N.C., U.S.A. 43 H5
Newton, N.J., U.S.A. 42 E8
Newton, Tex., U.S.A. 41 K8
Newton Abbot 9 G4
Newton Aycliffe 8 C6
Newton Stewart 10 G4
Newtonmore 10 D4
Newtown 9 E4
Newtownabbey 11 B6
Newtownards 11 B6
Newtownstewart 11 B4
Neyshābūr 24 B4
Nezperce 38 C5
Ngapara 33 L3
Ngoring Hu 20 C4
Nha Trang 23 B2
Nhill 32 C3
Niagara Falls, Canada 37 E12
Niagara Falls, U.S.A. 42 D6
Niamey 26 F6
Nias 23 C1
Nicaragua ■ 44 E7
Nicaragua, L. de 44 E7
Nice 12 E7
Niceville 43 K2
Nicholasville 42 G3
Nicobar Is. 25 E8
Nicosia 17 C4
Nicoya, Pen. de 44 F7
Nidd → 8 D6
Niedersachsen □ 16 B4
Niemen = Nemunas → 18 D3
Niger ■ 26 E7
Niger → 26 G7
Nigeria ■ 26 G7
Nightcaps 33 L2
Niigata 22 E6
Nijmegen 16 C2
Nikiniki 23 D4
Nikolayevsk-na-Amur 19 D15
Nikumaroro 31 A16
Nikunau 31 A14
Nîl, Nahr en → 27 B12
Nîl el Abyad → 27 E12
Nîl el Azraq → 27 E12
Nile = Nîl, Nahr en → 27 B12
Niles 42 E2
Nîmes 12 E6
Nimmitabel 32 C4
Nindigully 32 A4
Ninepin Group 21 G11
Ningbo 21 D7
Ningjing Shan 20 D4
Ningxia Huizu Zizhiqu □ 20 C5
Niobrara 40 D6
Niobrara → 40 D6
Niort 12 C3
Nipawin 36 D9
Nipigon, L. 37 E11
Nipissing, L. 37 E12
Nipomo 39 J3
Niš 15 C9
Nishinomiya 22 F4
Niterói 47 H10
Nith → 10 F5
Nitra 16 D9
Nitra → 16 E9
Niua Group 31 D16
Niuafo'ou 33 B11
Niuatoputapu 31 D16
Niue 31 D17
Niulakita 31 C14
Niutao 31 B14
Nivernais 12 C5
Nixa 41 G8
Nixon 41 L6
Nizamabad 25 D6
Nizhnevartovsk 18 C8
Nizhniy Novgorod 18 D5
Nizhniy Tagil 18 D6
Nízké Tatry 16 D9
Nizwá 24 C4
Nkongsamba 28 D1
Nobeoka 22 G2
Noblesville 42 E3
Nocona 41 J6
Nogales, Mexico 44 A2
Nogales, U.S.A. 39 L8
Noirmoutier, Î. de 12 C2
Nome 36 C3
Nord-Ostsee-Kanal 16 A4
Nordfriesische Inseln 16 A4
Nordkapp 7 C9
Nordrhein-Westfalen □ 16 C3
Nordvik 19 B12
Nore → 11 D4
Norfolk, Canada 42 D5
Norfolk, Nebr., U.S.A. 40 D6
Norfolk, Va., U.S.A. 42 G7
Norfolk □ 9 E8
Norfolk Basin 31 G13
Norfolk I. 31 F12
Norfolk Ridge 34 K8
Norfork L. 41 G8
Norilsk 19 C9
Normal 40 E10
Norman 41 H6
Norman Wells 36 C7
Normandie 12 B4
Normanton 30 D7
Norristown 42 E8
Norrköping 7 F7
Norrland 7 E7
Norseman 30 G3
North, C. 37 E13
North Adams 42 D9
North America 2 B5
North Atlantic Ocean 2 C8
North Augusta 43 J5
North Australian Basin 30 C2
North Ayrshire □ 10 F4
North Battleford 36 D9
North Bay 37 E12
North Bend 38 E1
North Berwick 10 E6
North C. 33 F4
North Canadian → 41 H7
North Cape = Nordkapp 7 C9
North Carolina □ 43 H6
North Cascades △ 38 B3
North Channel 10 F3
North Charleston 43 J6
North Chicago 42 D2
North Dakota □ 40 B5
North Downs 9 F8
North East Lincolnshire □ 8 D7
North Esk → 10 E6
North European Plain 3 B12
North Foreland 9 F9
North Fork Grand → 40 C3
North Fork Red → 41 H5
North I. 33 H5
North Korea ■ 21 C7
North Lanarkshire □ 10 F5
North Las Vegas 39 H6
North Lincolnshire □ 8 D7
North Little Rock 41 H8
North Loup → 40 E5
North Magnetic Pole 37 B9
North Mankato 40 C8
North Minch 10 C3
North Myrtle Beach 43 J6
North Palisade 39 H4
North Platte 40 E4
North Platte → 40 E4
North Pole 6 A
North Powder 38 D5
North Pt. 45 g
North Ronaldsay 10 B6
North Saskatchewan → 36 D9
North Sea 3 B10
North Somerset □ 9 F5
North Taranaki Bight 33 H5
North Thompson → 36 D7
North Tonawanda 42 D6
North Tyne → 8 B5
North Uist 10 D1
North Vernon 42 F3
North Walsham 8 E9
North West C. 30 E1
North West Frontier □ 25 B6
North West Highlands 10 D4
North West River 37 D13
North Wildwood 42 F8
North York Moors 8 C7
North Yorkshire □ 8 C6
Northallerton 8 C6
Northam 30 G2
Northampton, U.K. 9 E7
Northampton, U.S.A. 42 D9
Northamptonshire □ 9 E7
Northeast Pacific Basin 35 D13
Northern Ireland □ 11 B5
Northern Marianas ⊠ 34 F6
Northern Territory □ 30 E5
Northfield 40 C8
Northland □ 33 F4
Northome 40 B7
Northport, Ala., U.S.A. 43 J2
Northport, Wash., U.S.A. 38 B5
Northumberland □ 8 B6
Northumberland, C. 32 C3
Northumberland Str. 37 E13
Northwest Pacific Basin 34 D8
Northwest Territories □ 36 C8
Northwich 8 D5
Northwood, Iowa, U.S.A. 40 D8
Northwood, N. Dak., U.S.A. 40 B6
Norton 40 F5
Norton Sd. 36 C3
Norwalk, Conn., U.S.A. 42 E9
Norwalk, Iowa, U.S.A. 40 E8
Norwalk, Ohio, U.S.A. 42 E4
Norway, Maine, U.S.A. 43 C10
Norway, Mich., U.S.A. 42 C2
Norway ■ 7 E6
Norway House 36 D10
Norwegian B. 37 B9
Norwegian Sea 4 A9
Norwich, U.K. 9 E9
Norwich, Conn., U.S.A. 42 E9
Norwich, N.Y., U.S.A. 42 D8
Noss Hd. 10 C5
Nossob → 29 K4
Notre Dame B. 37 E14
Nottaway → 37 D12
Nottingham 8 E6
Nottingham I. 37 C12
Nottinghamshire □ 8 D6
Nottoway → 42 G7
Nouâdhibou 26 D2
Nouâdhibou, Ras 26 D2
Nouakchott 26 E2
Nouméa 31 E12
Nouvelle Amsterdam, Î. 5 F14
Nova Friburgo 47 H10
Nova Iguaçu 48 A8
Nova Scotia □ 37 E13
Novara 12 D8
Novaya Zemlya 18 B6
Novgorod 18 D4
Novi Sad 15 B8
Novocherkassk 17 A6
Novokuznetsk 18 D9
Novomoskovsk 18 D4
Novorossiysk 17 B5
Novoshakhtinsk 17 A5
Novosibirsk 18 D9
Novosibirskiye Ostrova 19 B15
Novotroitsk 18 D6
Nowata 41 G7
Nowra 32 B5
Nu Jiang → 20 D4
Nu Shan 20 D4
Nûbîya, Es Sahrâ en 27 D12
Nueces → 41 M6
Nueltin L. 36 C10
Nueva Rosita 44 B4
Nuevitas 45 C9
Nuevo Laredo 44 B5
Nugget Pt. 33 M2
Nuhaka 33 H6
Nui 31 B14
Nukey Bluff 32 B2
Nuku Hiva 35 H13
Nuku'alofa 33 E12
Nukulaelae 31 B14
Nukunonu 31 B16
Nukus 18 E6
Nullarbor Plain 30 G4
Numalla, L. 32 A3
Numazu 22 F6
Numurkah 32 C4
Nunap Isua 6 D4
Nunavut □ 37 C11
Nuneaton 9 E6
Nunivak I. 36 D3
Nuremberg = Nürnberg 16 D5
Nuriootpa 32 B2
Nürnberg 16 D5
Nushki 24 C5
Nuuk 6 C4
Nuweveldberge 29 L4
Nuyts Arch. 32 B1
Nyainqentanglha Shan 20 D4
Nyasa, L. = Malawi, L. 29 G6
Nymagee 32 B4
Nymboida △ 32 A5
Nyngan 32 B4
Nysa 16 C8
Nyssa 38 E5

O

Oa, Mull of 10 F2
Oacoma 40 D5
Oahe, L. 40 C4
Oahe Dam 40 C4
Oak Harbor 38 B2
Oak Hill 42 G5
Oak Island 43 J6
Oak Ridge 43 G3
Oakdale 41 K8
Oakes 40 B5
Oakesdale 38 C5
Oakey 32 A5
Oakham 9 E7
Oakland 39 H2
Oakley, Idaho, U.S.A. 38 E7
Oakley, Kans., U.S.A. 40 F4
Oakridge 38 E2
Oamaru 33 L3
Oates Land 6 D15
Oatlands 32 D4
Oaxaca 44 D5
Ob → 18 C7
Oba 37 E11
Oban 10 E3
Obbia 24 E3
Oberhausen 16 C3
Oberlin, Kans., U.S.A. 40 F4
Oberlin, La., U.S.A. 41 K8
Oberon 32 B4
Obi 23 D4
Obihiro 22 B8
Obskaya Guba 18 C8
Ocala 43 L4
Occidental, Cordillera 46 C3
Ocean City, Md., U.S.A. 42 F8
Ocean City, N.J., U.S.A. 42 F8
Ocean Park 38 C1
Oceanside 39 K5
Ochil Hills 10 E5
Ocho Rios 44 a
Ocilla 43 K4
Ocmulgee → 43 K4
Oconee → 43 K4
Oconomowoc 40 D10
Oconto 42 C2
Oconto Falls 42 C1
Odawara 22 F6
Odense 7 F6
Oder → 16 B7
Odesa 17 A4
Odessa, Tex., U.S.A. 41 K3
Odessa, Wash., U.S.A. 38 C4
O'Donnell 41 J4
Oelrichs 40 D3
Oelwein 40 D9
Oeno I. 35 K14
Offa 26 G6
Offaly □ 11 C4
Offenbach 16 C4
Ogaden 24 E3
Ōgaki 22 F5
Ogallala 40 E4
Ogasawara Gunto 34 E6
Ogbomosho 26 G6
Ogden 38 F7
Ogdensburg 42 C8
Ogeechee → 43 K5
Ogooué → 28 E1
Ohai 33 L2
Ohakune 33 H5
Ohau, L. 33 L2
Ohio □ 42 E3
Ohio → 42 G1
Ohře → 16 C7
Ohridsko Jezero 15 D9
Oil City 42 E6
Oise → 12 B5
Oistins 45 g
Oistins B. 45 g
Ōita 22 G2
Ojai 39 J4
Ojos del Salado, Cerro 48 B3
Oka → 18 D5
Okahandja 29 J3
Okanogan 38 B4
Okanogan → 38 B4
Okavango Delta 29 H4
Okayama 22 F3
Okazaki 22 F5
Okeechobee 43 M5
Okeechobee, L. 43 M5
Okefenokee △ 43 K4
Okefenokee Swamp 43 K4
Okehampton 9 G4
Okha 19 D15
Okhotsk 19 D15
Okhotsk, Sea of 19 D15
Okinawa-Jima 21 D7
Oklahoma □ 41 H6
Oklahoma City 41 H6
Okmulgee 41 H7
Okolona 41 J10
Oktyabrskoy Revolyutsii, Ostrov 19 B10
Okuru 33 K2
Ola 41 H8
Olancha 39 H4
Öland 7 F7
Olary 32 B3

55

 **AFGHANISTAN**
 ALBANIA
 ALGERIA
 ANDORRA
 ANGOLA
 ANTIGUA & BARBUDA
 ARGENTINA

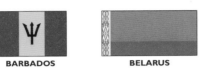 **BARBADOS**
 BELARUS
 BELGIUM
 BELIZE
 BENIN
 **BHUTAN**
 BOLIVIA

 BURUNDI
 CAMBODIA
 **CAMEROON**
 **CANADA**
 **CAPE VERDE**
 **CENTRAL AFRICAN REP.**
 CHAD

 **CROATIA**
 **CUBA**
 CYPRUS
 CZECH REPUBLIC
 DENMARK
 DJIBOUTI
 DOMINICA

 **ESTONIA**
 **ETHIOPIA**
 **FIJI ISLANDS**
 **FINLAND**
 **FRANCE**
 GABON
 GAMBIA

 **GUINEA**
 **GUINEA-BISSAU**
 **GUYANA**
 **HAITI**
 **HONDURAS**
 HUNGARY
 **ICELAND**

 IVORY COAST
 **JAMAICA**
 JAPAN
 **JORDAN**
 **KAZAKHSTAN**
 KENYA
 **KIRIBATI**

 **LESOTHO**
 **LIBERIA**
 LIBYA
 **LIECHTENSTEIN**
 LITHUANIA
 LUXEMBOURG
 MACEDONIA

 MARSHALL ISLANDS
 **MAURITANIA**
 MAURITIUS
 **MEXICO**
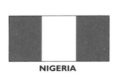 **MICRONESIA**
 MOLDOVA
 MONACO

 NEW ZEALAND
 NICARAGUA
 **NIGER**
 **NIGERIA**
 NORTHERN MARIANAS
 NORWAY
 OMAN

 PORTUGAL
 **PUERTO RICO**
 QATAR
 **ROMANIA**
 **RUSSIA**
 RWANDA
 SAMOA

 **SINGAPORE**
 **SLOVAK REPUBLIC**
 **SLOVENIA**
 **SOLOMON ISLANDS**
 **SOMALIA**
 SOUTH AFRICA
 **SPAIN**

 SWEDEN
 SWITZERLAND
 SYRIA
 TAIWAN
 TAJIKISTAN
 TANZANIA
 THAILAND

 UGANDA
 UKRAINE
 **UNITED ARAB EMIRATES**
 **UNITED KINGDOM**
 **UNITED STATES**
 URUGUAY
 UZBEKISTAN